TRUSTING IN THE NAMES OF GOD

CATHERINE MARTIN

HARVEST HOUSE PUBLISHERS

EUGENE, OREGON

TRUSTING IN THE NAMES OF GOD—A QUIET TIME EXPERIENCE
Copyright © 2008 by Catherine Martin
Published by Harvest House Publishers
Eugene, Oregon 97402
www.harvesthousepublishers.com

ISBN-13: 978-0-7369-2354-5
ISBN-10: 0-7369-2354-3

Printed in the United States of America

08 09 10 11 12 13 14 15 16 / ML-NI / 10 9 8 7 6 5 4 3 2 1

To Vonette Z. Bright,

cofounder of Campus Crusade for Christ,
an amazing woman of faith,
and my friend.

You have shown me how to trust God,
and your example shines as a light in this world.

—⁂—

Many daughters have done nobly,
But you excel them all
Proverbs 31:29

One thing I have asked from the LORD, that I shall seek:
That I may dwell in the house of the LORD all the days of my life,
To behold the beauty of the LORD and to meditate in His temple.

PSALM 27:4

⁓

And those who know Your name will put their trust in You.

PSALM 9:10

⁓

This is what the LORD says, "…let those who boast, boast about this:
that they understand and know me."

JEREMIAH 9:24 TNIV

⁓

Some boast in chariots and some in horses,
But we will boast in the name of the LORD, our God.

PSALM 20:7

❧ CONTENTS ❧

≫◦ INTRODUCTION ◦≪

Amy Carmichael walked leisurely along the road one Sunday morning after enjoying a church service in a beautiful, fashionable church. Suddenly she noticed a forlorn, old woman carrying a heavy bundle. Without thinking, Amy rushed over to help the woman. But then she thought, *What if people see me with this woman? What will they think?* An immediate wrestling in her mind about the eternal values in one's life work and the importance of things that last forever brought her to a point of decision.

A passage of Scripture came to her mind, "If any man build upon this foundation gold, silver, precious stones, wood, hay, stubble; every man's work shall be made manifest: for the day shall declare it, because it shall be revealed by fire; and the fire shall try every man's work, of what sort it is. If any man's work abide which he hath built thereupon, he shall receive a reward" (1 Corinthians 3:12-14 KJV). In an instant, Amy made a decision that altered the course of her life—she decided to live for eternal things, for things that last forever. In that defining moment, she decided that knowing God, living for Him, and pleasing Him were the only things that mattered, and temporal pleasures and earthly attention possessed no value in God's economy. She summed up her new resolve with these words: "Nothing could ever matter again but the things that were eternal."[1]

When you read any of Amy Carmichael's 35 books, you discover woven throughout her writings the theme of the eternal, those things that last forever. Amy Carmichael set aside many things for "the one thing"—knowing God. He was more important to her than everything else in her life. Her love for Him is the only explanation for her radical action in her day to leave the comforts of home and family in Northern Ireland at the age of 29 and minister to orphans and others in India for 55 years. She is an example of those who have been willing to "no longer live for themselves, but for Him who died and rose again on their behalf" (2 Corinthians 5:15).

She would often travel long distances on hot, dusty roads to save a suffering child. In 1931 she suffered a fall and was badly injured, and she was bedridden for most of the last 20 years of her life. Yet even in those long years, shut in and lonely, she used her time to write many of the books others have learned from and loved. Amy Carmichael is a great hero of the faith who breathed the air of heaven and soared above the clouds of life's difficult circumstances. Her life has been an inspiration to many who have served the Lord on the mission field, including Elisabeth and Jim Elliot.

How can you live a life of eternal significance and invest in treasure that lasts forever? How can you become an inspiration and influence to those around you? How can you walk with purpose in a world that is madly rushing nowhere? The answer to these questions is to trust in the names of God. Knowing God's names and then living out your life by what you know to be true is the key that unlocks the door to the spiritual world of things that last forever.

We all must decide how to spend our lives. And once our days are spent, those days are gone. No wonder the Lord says we need to be careful how we walk, making the most of our time (Ephesians 5:15-16). Now is the moment of decision to live for what lasts forever: knowing, loving, and trusting God. The good news is that once you make that most important decision, regardless of your age, God will reveal Himself to you and do great and mighty things in His name and for His glory. You will step into the unfathomable river of His plans and purposes. And oh, how exciting your life will become on the great adventure of knowing God!

I invite you to join me in a life-changing experience, one that begins with a verse written by David, the man after God's own heart. God gave me this verse 30 years ago to guide my life and to set me on a great pursuit—to know Him. I challenge you to join Amy Carmichael and me in setting aside many good things for the best thing—knowing God. Why must you set aside many good things? Because those good things sometimes eat up all the time you have in life, set you on the fast lane, and dominate every ounce of your being, leaving no time or energy to slow down, sit with the Lord, and know Him.

I am often asked, "Why don't people spend more time in God's Word?" My response is this: "We are simply too busy." We can't go live in a monastery, as appealing as that idea might sometimes sound. So, what is the answer? Create space for God. Stop and look at your life and determine resolutely where and when you can be still, and know that He is God (Psalm 46:10 NIV). Our time together is going to help you do exactly that.

And so, dear friend, I am excited to begin this adventure with you. We will visit some of my favorite passages of Scripture and favorite characters in the Bible. This quiet time experience is designed for those who have busy lives but recognize that quiet time with God is essential for those who would experience His best and live for His glory. Knowing the Lord intimately requires spending time in His Word and in prayer.

This eight-week quiet time experience is the companion to the 30-day journey of *Trusting in the Names of God,* my book on the names of God, which defines their value and importance, offers a plan for trusting the names of God, and gives an in-depth look at 14 of the names of God. These two books complement each other, and using them both will promote the richest growth and understanding of knowing God and His names.

You will discover that in this quiet time experience, all you need is your Bible and this book for a rich time alone with the Lord. It is filled with devotional readings, devotional Bible studies, hymns, journal pages, prayers, and practical applications. It is more than a simple devotional and more than a Bible study. Each quiet time is organized according to the PRAYER Quiet Time Plan:

Prepare Your Heart

Read and Study God's Word

Adore God in Prayer

Yield Yourself to God

Enjoy His Presence

Rest in His Love

Each week consists of five days of quiet times and then a devotional reading on days 6–7. Journal and prayer pages (adapted from the *Quiet Time Notebook*) are included in the back of this book for your use during these quiet times. Companion messages are available on the *Trusting in the Names of God DVD* from Quiet Time Ministries. Use the discussion questions in the back of this book if you are using this book with a friend or a group. If you desire to learn more about how to have a quiet time, I encourage you to get my book *Six Secrets to a Powerful Quiet Time.* To learn more about different kinds of devotional Bible studies for your quiet time, I encourage you to read my book *Knowing and Loving the Bible.*

As you begin these quiet times, I'd like to ask, where are you? What has been happening in your life over the past year or so? What has been your life experience? What are you facing, and what has God been teaching you? It is no accident that you are using this book of quiet times. In fact, God has something He wants you to know, something that will change the whole landscape of your experience with Him. Watch for it, listen for it, and when you learn it, write it down and never let it go.

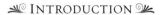

Will you write a prayer in the form of a letter to the Lord, expressing all that is on your heart and asking Him to speak to you in these quiet times?

My Letter to the Lord

Week One

A HEART FOR THE LORD

In this hour of all-but-universal darkness one cheering gleam appears: within the fold of conservative Christianity there are to be found increasing numbers of persons whose religious lives are marked by a hunger after God Himself. They are eager for spiritual realities and will not be put off with words, nor will they be content with correct "interpretations" of truth. They are athirst for God, and they will not be satisfied till they have drunk deep at the Fountain of Living Water.

A.W. TOZER

THE ONE THING

One thing I have asked…
PSALM 27:4

PREPARE YOUR HEART

When you read the Bible cover to cover, something stands out, especially if you've known and loved the Word for many years. As you move from page to page, you read of the lives of men and women who grappled with the deep questions of life: Who am I? Why am I here? What is life all about? These men and women struggled with trials, wrestled with God, and suffered through some very difficult relationships. This leads to three observations. First, as Alan Redpath says, "The Bible never flatters its heroes." These men and woman were average human beings you can identify with, possessing many flaws and walking with feet of clay. Second, you discover, woven through each life, the thread of God's invitation to know Him, the revelation of Himself through His names, and the subsequent response. Some drew near and trusted God, and others did not. But when a heart steps out of the crowd and draws near to God, He makes a big deal of it, as if throwing a ticker-tape parade from heaven. And third, He always displays the secret of each hero's life. And the secret was this: They had hearts for the Lord.

Look at Hezekiah, who "trusted in the LORD, the God of Israel; so that after him there was none like him among all the kings of Judah, nor among those who were before him. For he clung to the LORD; he did not depart from following Him, but kept His commandments, which the LORD had commanded Moses. And the LORD was with him; wherever he went he prospered" (2 Kings 18:5-7).

Look at Josiah. "There was no king like him who turned to the LORD with all his heart and with all his soul and with all his might, according to all the law of Moses" (2 Kings 23:25).

Look at David, whom God called "a man after My heart, who will do all My will" (Acts 13:22).

Dear friend, will you endeavor to have a heart for the Lord, one that knows Him and loves Him and trusts Him the way Hezekiah, Josiah, and David did? This week, we are going to discover some of the qualities that made David special and led God to call him "a man after My heart." There is no greater joy than to hear those words from God and to have a heart that distinguishes you from so many others. Ask the Lord now to quiet your heart and speak to you from His Word.

Read and Study God's Word

1. Today we are going to travel to the hymnbook of the Bible and read through one of David's best psalms, Psalm 27, which was written during a time of danger. Read Psalm 27 and record what is most significant to you.

2. Read Psalm 27:4 and write out all that David said he desired from the Lord.

3. Notice that David says, "One thing I have asked from the Lord." Those who have hearts for the Lord are clear about their purpose. They have a singular goal and pointed focus. Look at the following verses and record what you learn about the importance of your purpose and focus in life:

Luke 10:38-42

1 Corinthians 9:23-27

Philippians 3:8

Adore God in Prayer

Draw near to the Lord now and ask Him to give you a heart that longs to know Him. Ask Him to make you a person after His own heart.

YIELD YOURSELF TO GOD

One supreme desire occupies the believing heart. He longs for close communion with the Lord. He diligently uses all appointed means. He seeks the ordinances which God's presence sanctifies. Such is the constant habit of his soul. It is no transient impulse…His eyes would see the beauty of the Lord: the lovely charm of His transcendent grace, displayed in redemption's wondrous work. His soul thirsts after fuller knowledge. His ardent cry is *Show me Thy glory.*[1]

HENRY LAW

ENJOY HIS PRESENCE

F.B. Meyer says, "'One thing' people are irresistible."[2] And is this not true? Will you resolve to be a "one thing" person today? Close your time with the Lord by writing a prayer of commitment to Him to be a "one thing" person, wholeheartedly devoted to Him.

REST IN HIS LOVE

"Yes, indeed, I certainly do count everything as loss compared with the priceless privilege of knowing Christ Jesus my Lord" (Philippians 3:8 WILLIAMS).

SEEKING THE LORD

...that I shall seek...
PSALM 27:4

PREPARE YOUR HEART

Treasure hunters spend millions of dollars as well as years of their lives searching for billions of dollars of gold bullion beneath the seas. They devote their precious days to find diamonds, emeralds, priceless artifacts, and works of art lost in sunken ships or in forgotten caverns. Their dreams are wrapped up in the wishful promise of buried treasure. But a greater treasure awaits any man or woman of God who is willing to look—the magnificent riches of God Himself. He promises, "You will seek Me and find Me when you search for Me with all your heart" (Jeremiah 29:13). What an incredible promise. Today, as you begin your time with the Lord, meditate on the words of Psalm 105:1-7 and ask the Lord to show you how to seek Him with all your heart.

READ AND STUDY GOD'S WORD

1. Read the words of David in Psalm 27:4 again. What is your favorite part of this verse today and why?

2. We see in Psalm 27 that David sought one thing and desired it more than anything else. In short, David wanted to know and experience an intimate relationship with the Lord. The Hebrew word for "seek" is *darash* and means "to pursue with great care and concern." The Bible has a lot to say about seeking the Lord. Look at the following verses and record what you learn about seeking the Lord:

1 Chronicles 16:7-12

Psalm 27:8

Psalm 34:10

Proverbs 28:5

Isaiah 31:1

Isaiah 55:6

3. Summarize in two or three sentences what you have learned about seeking the Lord.

4. Why is seeking the Lord important if you want to know God and trust Him?

ADORE GOD IN PRAYER

My soul wakes early and turns to you, O God, for the light. Your light is better than life; therefore, my lips shall praise you. Take my hand in yours, and make the crooked places straight and the rough places plain, that your name may be glorified in my daily walk and conversation.[3]

F.B. MEYER

YIELD YOURSELF TO GOD

Our desires of the Lord should be sanctified, humble, constant, submissive, fervent, and it is well if, as with the psalmist, they are all molten into one mass. Under David's painful circumstances we might have expected him to desire repose, safety, and a thousand other good things, but no, he has set his heart on the pearl, and leaves the rest. That will I seek after. Holy desires must lead to resolute action. The old proverb says, "Wishers and woulders are never good housekeepers," and "Wishing never fills a sack." Desires are seed which must be sown in the good soil of activity, or they will yield no harvest. We shall find our desires to be like clouds without rain, unless followed up by practical endeavours.[4]

CHARLES SPURGEON

ENJOY HIS PRESENCE

What do you spend time pursuing with great care and concern? How do you spend the precious days entrusted to you by the Lord? Do you seek the Lord? What would lead you to seek the Lord more? Think about all you have learned today. Write your response to the Lord in the space provided.

REST IN HIS LOVE

"When You said, 'Seek My face,' my heart said to You, 'Your face, O LORD, I shall seek'" (Psalm 27:8).

LIVING WITH THE LORD

...that I may dwell in the house of the LORD all the days of my life...

PSALM 27:4

PREPARE YOUR HEART

The story is told of one who dreamed of walking with the Lord on the beach. During their walk, events from life flashed across the sky that included footprints in the sand. Sometimes two sets of footprints revealed a walk with the Lord through the daily events of life. But in the most difficult times, only one set of footprints was evident in the sand. Struggling to understand, the traveler asked the Lord why, during the most difficult times, He would leave. The Lord responded that He never left but rather carried His precious servant.

We have been looking at David's tremendous heart for the Lord. More than anything he wanted to "dwell in the house of the LORD" all the days of his life. In his day, the house of the Lord represented the presence of the Lord. What David really wanted was to live in the Lord's presence, experience an intimate relationship with the Lord, and enjoy Him every day of his life. In short, David wanted to know God.

As you think about your life today, what is your focus? Is your life wrapped up in this world— houses, cars, clothes, shopping, and entertainment—or is your life wrapped up in the Lord? Where are your thoughts most of the time? Do you think about the Lord and talk with Him throughout the day? Or do you go through your day hardly giving the Lord a thought or a prayer at all? Is knowing God your heart's desire?

As you begin your quiet time, think about those footprints in the sand. Ask the Lord if you may "dwell in His house" all the days of your life, walking with Him every moment of the day.

READ AND STUDY GOD'S WORD

1. David teaches us that it is good to desire to live with the Lord. How is this life possible? Moses referred to God as our "dwelling place." Underline your favorite phrases in each translation of Deuteronomy 33:27 below.

"The eternal God is a dwelling place, and underneath are the everlasting arms."

"The everlasting God is your place of safety, and his arms will hold you up forever" (NCV).

"The eternal God is your refuge, and underneath are the everlasting arms" (NIV).

2. What is your favorite truth about your God in that verse?

3. Read Psalm 37:23 in the following translations and underline the phrases that mean the most to you.

"The steps of a man are established by the LORD, and He delights in his way."

"The LORD makes firm the steps of those who delight in him" (TNIV).

"When a person's steps follow the LORD, God is pleased with his ways" (NCV).

"The LORD directs the steps of the godly. He delights in every detail of their lives" (NLT).

4. What is your favorite phrase in the different translations of Psalm 37:23?

5. Read Psalm 1 and write all that you learn about those who are blessed in life.

6. What have you learned about the Lord today that will help you in your life with Him?

ADORE GOD IN PRAYER

Take some time now to talk with the Lord about your life with Him. Ask Him to give you a heart for Him, and tell Him how much you desire to walk with Him each day.

YIELD YOURSELF TO GOD

But our God is the tried, the proved God of His people. His Word has been tried, and proved divine. His promises have been tried, and proved true. His veracity has been tried, and proved faithful. His love has been tried, and proved unchangeable. His compassion has been tried, and proved real. In a word, His children can all testify, by personal, holy, and loving experience, that God is all that His revealed Word declares Him to be, and that the Lord Jesus is all that the prophet declares Him to be—the "Tried Stone" for sinners to build upon, and for saints to trust in.

Oh, the blessedness of knowing that this prayer-hearing, prayer-answering, and prayer-exceeding God; this promise-making and promise-keeping God; this love-unchanging, and covenant-keeping God is "our God!" What encouragement have we to deal personally, constantly, and closely with our God in all the circumstances and events of daily life! We repair to Him in need, in difficulty, and in trial, in the firm persuasion that in the history of His Church He has proved all that we now require Him to be; that all that He has been He is now; and that what other saints have found Him in their experience we shall find Him in ours.[5]

OCTAVIUS WINSLOW

ENJOY HIS PRESENCE

Think about the time you have taken to pack and move into a house or an apartment. And now, think about what it will take to move to that spiritual place in your life where you are living with the Lord and walking with Him day by day. What decisions and commitments can you make today to live with your Lord and walk with Him moment by moment? Write your thoughts in the space provided.

REST IN HIS LOVE

"The LORD makes firm the steps of those who delight in him; though they stumble, they will not fall, for the LORD upholds them with his hand" (Psalm 37:23-24 TNIV).

LOOKING AT HIS BEAUTY

...to behold the beauty of the LORD...
PSALM 27:4

PREPARE YOUR HEART

Have you ever been overwhelmed at the magnificence of a sunset? Or amazed at the power of the ocean waves crashing onto the sandy beach? Or stunned at the intricate detail of a rose just opening up in full bloom? The word often used for such views is *beauty*. Beauty is defined by Webster's dictionary as "the quality present in a thing or a person that gives intense pleasure or deep satisfaction to the mind."

David's great desire was to "behold the beauty of the LORD." The Hebrew word for "beauty" is *noam* and means "goodness or kindness." Translators have used the words "loveliness of the Lord" (Anchor Bible Commentary Series) or "the sweetness of Yahweh" (New Jerusalem Bible). David's words reveal his great desire. He did not just want to talk about God. He did not want to watch others experience God. David wanted to enjoy God firsthand. He wanted to "behold" or look with awe at all the facets of God.

How can you behold the beauty of the Lord? By knowing and trusting His names. God has progressively displayed many facets of His beauty through His names. When He revealed a name for Himself in biblical times, He always did so with purpose, to explain who He is, what He does, and what He says. The result of knowing and trusting God's names is a more intimate relationship with God.

As you draw near to God today, ask Him to reveal Himself to you so that you might behold His beauty.

READ AND STUDY GOD'S WORD

1. Today you are considering the beauty of the Lord. Look at the following translations of Psalm 27:4 and note the different ways "beauty of the Lord" is translated. Underline the phrases in each translation that describe David's great desire to behold the beauty of the Lord.

"One thing I have asked from the LORD, that I shall seek: that I may dwell in the house of the LORD all the days of my life, To behold the beauty of the LORD and to meditate in His temple."

"I have asked the LORD for one thing—this is what I desire! I want to live in the LORD's house all the days of my life, so I can gaze at the splendor of the LORD and contemplate in his temple" (NET).

"The one thing I ask of the LORD—the thing I seek most—is to live in the house of the LORD all the days of my life, delighting in the LORD's perfections and meditating in his Temple" (NLT).

"I'm asking God for one thing, only one thing: To live with him in his house my whole life long. I'll contemplate his beauty; I'll study at his feet" (MSG).

2. How can you behold God's amazing beauty? Through His names. Like the facets of a diamond, God's character shines with brilliance as He pours His light onto His names. Whenever God reveals one of His names to you, He is showing you something about His character and His ways. His names are not mere identification tags; rather, they represent who God is and draw you into a more intimate relationship with Him. And the more you know Him, the more you will trust Him. Look at the following verses and record what you learn about the names of God.

Deuteronomy 32:3-4

Psalm 9:10

Proverbs 18:10

3. Summarize what you have learned about the benefits of knowing the names of God.

revealing his character to us

ADORE GOD IN PRAYER

Turn to Psalm 27 and use the words of David to talk with the Lord, thanking Him for who He is and what He does. You might begin like this: *Lord, You are my light and my salvation. Whom shall I fear? You are the defense of my life...*

YIELD YOURSELF TO GOD

When we lift our inward eyes to gaze upon God we are sure to meet friendly eyes gazing back at us, for it is written that the eyes of the Lord run to and fro throughout the earth. The sweet language of experience is "Thou God seest me." When the eyes of the soul looking out meet the eyes of God looking in, heaven has begun right here on this earth...Private prayer should be practiced by every Christian. Long periods of Bible meditation will purify our gaze and direct it; church attendance will enlarge our outlook and increase our love for others. Service and work and activity; all are good and should be engaged in by every Christian. But at the bottom of all these things, giving meaning to them, will be the inward habit of beholding God. A new set of eyes (so to speak) will develop within us enabling us to be looking at God while our outward eyes are seeing the scenes of this passing world.[6]

A.W. TOZER

ENJOY HIS PRESENCE

Think about how you have beheld the beauty of the Lord recently, perhaps in the last year or so. What have you learned about God? How has what you have learned impacted your relationship with Him? Describe what you learned about Him and how your discoveries of God have made a difference in your life.

REST IN HIS LOVE

"The name of the LORD is a strong tower; the righteous runs into it and is safe" (Proverbs 18:10).

LEARNING ABOUT HIS WAYS

...and to meditate in His temple...
PSALM 27:4

PREPARE YOUR HEART

F.B. Meyer, a busy pastor and prolific writer, preached in England at the same time the popular G. Campbell Morgan and Charles Spurgeon occupied pulpits nearby. Near the end of his life, he described his personal relationship with the Lord over the years as "the constant interchange between Him and me."[7] F.B. Meyer loved to study God's Word and was a scholar, a brilliant thinker, and a prolific writer. He wrote more than 50 books, including autobiographies, biographies, devotionals, and commentaries. He did not just read the Word, he thought about it, got personal with God about it, and then expounded it with a unique style blending teaching with practical application in daily living.

Have you learned to think about what God says in His Word? David wanted not only to behold the beauty of the Lord but also to "meditate in His temple." The Hebrew for "meditate" is *baqar* and means "to consider and reflect." Discovery of the greatest treasures of God requires time, study, and reflection in God's Word. Will you create space for God in your life and time with the Bible that you might know the Lord and His ways? Ask the Lord to speak to you from His Word today.

READ AND STUDY GOD'S WORD

1. David had a habit of spending time with his Lord. His time was well spent, for it gave him a heart for the Lord. He loved to sit in the Lord's presence and did it often, from the time he was a shepherd of sheep to the time when he was king of Israel. Read his words in 2 Samuel 7:18-24 and record everything David learned about himself and about the Lord when "he went in and sat before the LORD."

2. Moses shared David's desire to know God and behold His beauty. Read what Moses said to God in Exodus 33:13-14. Write out what Moses wanted and how the Lord responded.

3. As you think about David and Moses, describe in your own words what it means to have a heart for the Lord.

4. What have you learned from David and Moses that will help you to have a heart for the Lord?

ADORE GOD IN PRAYER

Pray using the words of Psalm 86:11-12:

Teach me Your way, O LORD;
I will walk in Your truth;
Unite my heart to fear Your name.
I will give thanks to You, O Lord my God, with all my heart,
And will glorify Your name forever.

YIELD YOURSELF TO GOD

This God, who has made such a divine and wonderful revelation of Himself—His Being and mind, His will and heart; in His word, is, "our God." In other words, the God of the Bible is ours. All that that inspired and precious volume declares concerning Him, all the thoughts of His mind it reveals, all the love of His nature it makes known, all the teaching of His Spirit it conveys, all the precious promises, all the gracious invitations, and the glorious hopes, and solemn warnings and faithful admonitions it contains, are ours, because the God of the Bible is ours. Accept the Bible as your own. Read it as the letters of your Heavenly Father addressed personally to you. Let no sophistry shake your confidence in its divine inspiration. Beware of that false reasoning that teaches that God's Word is in the Bible, but that the Bible is not God's Word. The giant evil of the day is infidelity unblushingly assailing the truth, and impeaching the integrity of the Sacred Scriptures. Be vigilant and prayerful here. Lose your Bible, and you lose your all. If, then, the God of revelation is yours, the revelation of God is equally yours. All that this blessed volume contains belongs of a right to you. The Divine Redeemer, the glorious gospel, the free salvation, the precious promises, the gracious invitations, the rich consolations, the blissful hopes, the holy admonitions, all, all are ours, because the God who wrote the Bible, who gave the Bible, who has preserved the Bible, and who dwells in the Bible, is "our God."

May the hand of your faith [rest] upon this Divine Charter of blessings, and exclaim, "It is mine, all, all is mine, because the God who inspired it is my God. In giving me Himself He gave me all that was His and this is His most precious gift, next to His beloved Son, whom it reveals. Let me believe it firmly, deal with it reverently, read it devoutly, and walk in its divine precepts holily, and do all in my power to give to all who may not possess, as I do, this heavenly chart, this divine compass, this unerring light in the soul's solemn travel to eternity."[8]

OCTAVIUS WINSLOW

ENJOY HIS PRESENCE

Close your time with the Lord today thinking about this poem by John Burton:

> Holy Bible, book divine,
> Precious treasure, thou art mine;
> Mine to tell me whence I came;
> Mine to teach me what I am;
>
> Mine to chide me when I rove;
> Mine to show a Savior's love;
> Mine thou art to guide and guard;
> Mine to punish or reward;
>
> Mine to comfort in distress,
> Suffering in this wilderness;
> Mine to show, by living faith,
> Man can triumph over death;

Mine to tell of joys to come,
And the rebel sinner's doom;
O thou holy book divine,
Precious treasure, thou art mine!

REST IN HIS LOVE

"Let me know Your ways that I may know You" (Exodus 33:13).

DEVOTIONAL READING
BY F.B. MEYER

As day after day [David] considered the heavens and earth, they appeared as one vast tent, in which God dwelt. Nature was the material dwelling-place of the eternal Spirit, who was as real to his young heart as the works of His hands to His poet's eyes. God was as real to him as Jesse, or his brothers, or Saul, or Goliath. His soul had so rooted itself in this conception of God's presence, that he bore it with him, undisturbed by the shout of the soldiers as they went forth to the battle, and the searching questions addressed to him by Saul. This is the unfailing secret. There is no short cut to the life of faith, which is the all-vital condition of a holy and victorious life. We must have periods of lonely meditation and fellowship with God. That our souls should have their mountains of fellowship, their valleys of quiet rest beneath the shadow of a great rock, their nights beneath the stars, when darkness has veiled the material and silenced the stir of human life, and has opened the view of the infinite and eternal, is as indispensable as that our bodies should have food. Thus alone can the sense of God's presence become the fixed possession of the soul, enabling it to say repeatedly with the psalmist, "Thou art near, O God."[9]

Take some time now to write about all that you have learned this week regarding having a heart for the Lord. What has been most significant to you? Close by writing a prayer to the Lord.

TRUSTING IN THE LORD

It is not hard, you find, to trust the management of the universe, and of all the outward creation, to the Lord. Can your case then be so much more complex and difficult than these, that you need to be anxious or troubled about His management of you? Away with such unworthy doubtings! Take your stand on the power and trustworthiness of your God, and see how quickly all difficulties will vanish before a steadfast determination to believe. Trust in the dark, trust in the light, trust at night and trust in the morning, and you will find that the faith that may begin perhaps by a mighty effort, will end, sooner or later, by becoming the easy and natural habit of the soul.

HANNAH WHITALL SMITH

THE FOUNDATION OF TRUST

And those who know Your name will put their trust in You,
for You, O LORD, have not forsaken those who seek You.
PSALM 9:10

PREPARE YOUR HEART

When a good contractor builds a house, he pays great attention to the laying of a good strong foundation. When the foundation is solid, the house can withstand storms and even earthquakes. The same is true for you. Paying attention to the names of God and knowing His character in detail provides a strong foundation for you to grow and to trust God in your everyday life. When you know God is able and strong, you will run to Him for help. When you know He is good and kind and merciful, you will run to Him when you are hurt. When you know He is all-sufficient, possessing enough resources for anything you face today, tomorrow's storm won't seem nearly so overwhelming and burdensome. And you will trust Him in today's deep needs. How well do you know the names of God? Are you able to cry out to God about the burdens of your heart, addressing Him by many of His names and thanking Him for who He is and what He does?

How can you build a good strong foundation with the names of God? By opening the Word of God daily to discover His names. And this kind of commitment requires an evaluation of how you spend your time. A.C. Gaebelein, a great Bible expositor born in 1861, was often asked how he was able to travel and speak so much, edit a magazine, and write so many books. He always replied with these words: "I never wasted time."[1] He was devoted to studying God's Word and dedicated to knowing God.

Knowing the names of God opens up a whole new world of prayer, spiritual growth, and relying on God when you are seemingly without resources to meet your needs. Discovering God's names and then drawing near to His names will empower you to trust in Him.

Today, ask the Lord to speak to you about His names and show you how to trust in Him.

READ AND STUDY GOD'S WORD

1. David, our hero of trust who had a heart for the Lord, was well-versed in the names of God. God has given you access to some of David's journal, contained in Psalms, so you can know some of his deepest thoughts, hopes, fears, desires, and affirmations of faith. Above all, you can see his love for the Lord and his wealth of knowledge about his God. Today, our focus is on Psalm 9, thought to have been written later in David's life about some of his great victories, for the purpose of praising the Lord. Read Psalm 9 and write your most significant insight about God from this psalm.

2. Write out Psalm 9:10 word for word in the space provided, thinking about each phrase and word.

3. The Hebrew word for "trust" is *batach* and means to place your reliance or belief in a person or object. David is saying that when you know God's name, you will rely on Him and believe in Him. A good way to remember the meaning of TRUST is with the acrostic Total Reliance Under Stress and Trial. What ways do you need to trust God today, totally relying on Him under stress and trial?

4. Think about why the names of God are such a strong foundation for your trust in Him. Herbert Lockyer says that David's perspective of God's names emphasizes "all that God is in Himself, celebrates the confidence of those who know that name as if its fragrance still breathed in the atmosphere around."[2] Knowing the names of God breathes life into your trust and carries you through trial after trial on into eternity. Think about all that David learned about God through the years. He often referred to God's names in life's challenges. Look at the following verses and record what you learn about the relationship between knowing God's names and trusting in God:

1 Samuel 17:45-47

Psalm 44:4-8

Lamentations 3:52-58

Daniel 11:32

5. What is the most important truth you've learned about trusting in the names of God today?

6. Describe in your own words what a name of God represents and why knowing God's names helps you to trust in Him.

ADORE GOD IN PRAYER

Meditate on the words of this Puritan devotional prayer:

> Thou incomprehensible but prayer-hearing God,
> known, but beyond knowledge,
> revealed, but unrevealed,
> my wants and welfare draw me to thee,
> for thou hast never said, "Seek ye me in vain."
> To thee I come in my difficulties, necessities, distresses;
> possess me with thyself,
> with a spirit of grace and supplication,
> with a prayerful attitude of mind,
> with access into warmth of fellowship,
> so that in the ordinary concerns of life
> my thoughts and desires may rise to thee,

and in habitual devotion I may find a resource that will
soothe my sorrows, sanctify my successes,
and qualify me in all ways for dealings with my fellow men.
I bless thee that thou hast made me capable of knowing thee,
the author of all being
of resembling thee, the perfection of all excellency,
of enjoying thee, the source of all happiness.
O God, attend me in every part of my arduous and trying pilgrimage;
I need the same counsel, defense, comfort I found at my beginning.
Let my religion be more obvious to my conscience,
more perceptible to those around.
While Jesus is representing me in heaven, may I reflect him on earth,
while he pleads my cause, may I show forth his praise.
Continue the gentleness of thy goodness towards me.
And whether I wake or sleep, let thy presence go with me,
thy blessing attend me.
Thou hast led me on and I have found thy promises true,
I have been sorrowful, but thou hast been my help,
fearful, but thou hast delivered me,
despairing, but thou hast lifted me up.
Thy vows are ever upon me,
and I praise thee, O God.[3]

YIELD YOURSELF TO GOD

Meditate on these words by Charles Spurgeon, underlining the phrases that are most significant to you today:

"It is better to trust in the LORD than to put confidence in man" (Psalm 118:8). Doubtless the reader has been tried with the temptation to rely upon the things which are seen, instead of resting alone upon the invisible God. Christians often look to man for help and counsel, and mar the noble simplicity of their reliance upon their God...Is it not written, "Cast thy burden upon the Lord"? "Be careful for nothing, but in everything by prayer and supplication make known your wants unto God." Cannot you trust God for temporals? "*Ah! I wish I could.*" If you cannot trust God for temporals, how dare you trust him for spirituals? Can you trust him for your soul's redemption, and not rely upon him for a few lesser mercies? Is not God enough for thy need, or is his all-sufficiency too narrow for thy wants? Dost thou want another eye beside that of him who sees every secret thing? Is his heart faint? Is his arm weary? If so, seek another God; but if he be infinite, omnipotent, faithful, true, and all-wise, why gaddest thou abroad so much to seek another confidence? Why dost thou rake the earth to find another foundation, when this is strong enough to bear all the weight which thou canst ever build thereon?…Wait thou only upon God, and let thine expectation be from him. Covet not Jonah's gourd, but rest in Jonah's God. Let the sandy foundations of terrestrial trust be the choice of fools, but do thou, like one who foresees the storm, build for thyself an abiding place upon the Rock of Ages.[4]

ENJOY HIS PRESENCE

Dear friend, here is the great secret to think about and apply throughout this entire quiet time experience on trusting in the names of God: The foundation of your trust depends on knowing your God. And how can you know your God? By discovering His names in His Word. The more you know of God, the more you will trust Him. And is that not always so? You cannot trust whom you do not know. But when you know someone to be reliable, you are willing to trust him. And so it is with God. Will you take some time now to tell the Lord how much you want to know Him and then, as a result, how much you want to trust Him?

REST IN HIS LOVE

"The people who know their God will display strength and take action" (Daniel 11:32).

THE PRAYER OF TRUST

To You, O LORD, I lift up my soul.
O my God, in You I trust.
PSALM 25:1-2

PREPARE YOUR HEART

What is your first response when you are faced with a trial in your own life? The first and best offensive strike is to use the sword of the Spirit, which is the word of God, and a prayer of trust to your Lord. Paul says, "With all prayer and petition pray at all times in the Spirit, and with this in view, be on the alert with all perseverance and petition for all the saints" (Ephesians 6:18). No wonder David's psalms are filled with prayers of trust to his Lord. Over and over again, David cried out to the Lord for help and then declared what God was able to do. You must learn to do the same. Today we will look at words of trust by David. Ask God to show you how to pray like David in the heat of your trials.

READ AND STUDY GOD'S WORD

1. David wrote Psalm 25 late in life as he recalled his youth. One commentator calls this psalm a "true portrait of the writer's holy trust, his many trials, his great transgressions, his bitter repentance, and deep distresses—a true mark of a man after God's own heart, whose sorrows remind him of his sins, and whose sorrow for sin drives him to God."[5] Read these words of David and record your favorite verse or phrase. What is most significant to you today?

2. David was faced with challenges throughout his entire life—difficulties requiring a great trust in the Lord. David experienced a deep time of trouble when his own beloved son Absalom rebelled and betrayed him. Read 2 Samuel 15:1-6,10-13 and describe what Absalom did to betray his father, King David.

3. Such danger faced David from his son Absalom that David and his servants were forced to flee Jerusalem. Read 2 Samuel 15:25-31 and record all the ways David expressed TRUST (Total Reliance Under Stress and Trial) in the Lord.

4. Read Psalm 62:1-8, David's prayer of trust when surrounded by enemies, possibly even prayed when in danger from Absalom. What do you learn from his prayer that will help you pray a prayer of trust the next time you are in trouble?

ADORE GOD IN PRAYER

Turn to Psalm 25 and pray through verses 1-5, personalizing the words as a prayer from you to the Lord.

YIELD YOURSELF TO GOD

> True prayer is not formality. It is soul-work. In it the world and all its cares and vanities are left behind. Faith spreads rejoicing wings and soars above the heaven of heavens. The man of prayer lifts up his soul. It is faith's holy privilege to deal unreservedly with God: to open out its real condition: to call Him to witness that all vain confidences are renounced, and that all trust rests on Him. Such may fearlessly supplicate that no disappointments may cause shame; and that no foes may humble them. They who lift up the soul to God will lift up the head above all the fears of men.[6]
>
> HENRY LAW

ENJOY HIS PRESENCE

David affirmed his trust in God when he said, "In the LORD I put my trust" (Psalm 11:1 NKJV). Trust shines in the stormy environment. John Henry Jowett describes David's experience this way:

The sun is down. The stars are hid. The waters are out. The roads are broken up. And in the very midst of the darkness and desolation one hears the triumphant cry of the psalmist, "In the LORD put I my trust." The singer is a soul in difficulty. He is the victim of relentless antagonists. He is pursued by implacable foes. The fight would appear to be going against him. The enemies are overwhelming and, just at this point of seeming defeat and imminent disaster, there emerges this note of joyful confidence in God. "In the LORD put I my trust." It is a song in the night.[7]

Over and over again, throughout his prayers in Psalms, David expressed his trust in the Lord. Why is prayer such a wonderful demonstration of trust? What do you need to take to the Lord in prayer today in order to trust Him? Use the journal pages in the back of this book to write a prayer to Him.

REST IN HIS LOVE

"Trust in Him at all times, O people; pour out your heart before Him; God is a refuge for us" (Psalm 62:8).

THE TEST OF TRUST

My God, my God, why have You forsaken me?
Far from my deliverance are the words of my groaning.
O my God, I cry by day, but You do not answer;
and by night, but I have no rest.

PSALM 22:1-2

PREPARE YOUR HEART

Your trust in God will always be tested by the trial. The trial doesn't reveal what God will do. And therein lies the test. The trial threatens an outcome and seems to leave you completely without resource, and yet God promises resources and help from His heavenly direction. The secret is calculating God into your trial. How can you know about God, what He can do, and what He promises? Run to His Word. The Bible will give you the truth and reality about God: who He is, what He does, and what He says. Then you will depend on the names of God, leading you to trust in Him.

When Corrie ten Boom was a teenager, she witnessed the arrest and torture of another Christian. She was shocked and immediately thought about how she would respond in similar circumstances. She ran to her father and said, "I couldn't stand that. I would wilt under persecution. I'm afraid I wouldn't be faithful."

Her father responded, "Corrie, God will give you the faith you need."

"I don't have that kind of courage and faith," she insisted.

Finally her father said, "Do you remember when you were a little girl and we took rides on the train? I kept your ticket in my pocket. Do you remember when I gave you your ticket?"

"Yes, right before we got on the train," she replied.

"Right," he said. "I kept it until you needed it so you wouldn't lose it. God will give you the faith you need. He will empower you by His Holy Spirit according to your need. Trust Him for that."

Corrie indeed discovered firsthand the faithfulness of God to give her what she needed for the impossible suffering of Ravensbruck concentration camp. She saw God supply every need and carry her through the very darkest of all times. And He will do the same for you. In the trial that tests your trust, when God seems not to be there and to be silent, learn to calculate Him into your circumstance as the greatest factor of all and then watch to see what He will do.

Read Psalm 42:1-5 to prepare your heart and ask God to speak to you from His Word today.

READ AND STUDY GOD'S WORD

1. Our hero of trust, David, has written words expressing the deepest cries of a heart whose trust is tested. Psalm 22, sometimes called the psalm of the cross, appears to describe a crucifixion. No event in David's life can account for the words found here, and they are found in only one other place in the Bible. When Jesus was hanging on the cross, He cried out the words of Psalm 22:1: "My God, my God, why have You forsaken Me?" (Matthew 27:46). These words give us a view into the heart of our Lord Himself and help us understand the depth and darkness of suffering, the dark night of the soul, when we feel forsaken by God. Job felt this way when he cried out, "Though He slay me, yet will I trust Him" (Job 13:15 NKJV). And surely David also felt that God had forsaken him when he cried out, "How long, O LORD? Will You forget me forever?" (Psalm 13:1). To feel forsaken and yet to cry out to God is the greatest of all expressions of trust. Take some time to read through Psalm 22 and write out all the expressions of trust and prayers of trust you discover in this psalm.

2. How has your trust in God been tested? Where have you felt forsaken and forgotten? How can you calculate God into your circumstance today?

ADORE GOD IN PRAYER

Come to me, Lord, in my brokenness. My fair ideals are like trampled flowers, and my attempts after perfection have failed; but do for me what I cannot do for myself. Perfect that which concerns me, because your mercy endures forever.[8]

F.B. MEYER

YIELD YOURSELF TO GOD

> Sometimes to the soul in agony God seems not to hear; but through those hours of darkness the Easter day is hastening to break in resplendent glory. He will not suffer his holy one to see corruption (Psalm 16:10).[9]

F.B. MEYER

ENJOY HIS PRESENCE

Close your time today by writing a prayer of trust to your Lord using the journal pages in the back of this book.

REST IN HIS LOVE

"For He has not despised nor abhorred the affliction of the afflicted; nor has He hidden His face from him; but when he cried to Him for help, He heard" (Psalm 22:24).

THE RESULT OF TRUST

The LORD is my strength and my shield; my heart trusts in Him, and I am helped; therefore my heart exalts, and with my song I shall thank Him.

PSALM 28:7

PREPARE YOUR HEART

What happens when you trust in the Lord? He will help you—He promises. He is the Father of mercies, the God of all comfort, the God of hope, and so much more. We are about to embark on the most amazing adventure of discovering the names of God, His character, His attributes, His ways, and His works. When you see what He can do and what He promises, you will feel as though you suddenly became a millionaire because of all you possess in His promises of who He is. God is true to what He says—He keeps His promises. And each name of God is a promise He is making to you about who He is. When you trust what He promises about Himself, you will discover that He delivers on His promise. Then you will delight in His names, praising Him for who He is and what He has done in your life.

Today, as you draw near to God, where do you need help? Will you ask God for help today? Then watch to see what He does.

READ AND STUDY GOD'S WORD

1. Herbert Lockyer calls the words of David in Psalm 28 a "song in the night." And you must have songs in the night. You need His light for the times when all around you seems dark and yet you are confidently relying on your Lord, knowing He has heard your prayers. Sometimes when you have not yet heard from God, your heart finds the strength to trust Him even more, and you patiently keep on knocking as you have been instructed to do by Jesus Himself (Matthew 7:7-8). Read Psalm 28 and write what is most significant to you today about God in this psalm.

2. Look at the following translations of Psalm 28:7 and underline your favorite phrases and words.

"The LORD is my strength and my shield; my heart trusts in Him, and I am helped; therefore my heart exults, and with my song I shall thank Him."

"The LORD is my strength and shield. I trust him with all my heart. He helps me, and my heart is filled with joy. I burst out in songs of thanksgiving" (NLT).

"The LORD strengthens and protects me; I trust in him with all my heart. I am rescued and my heart is full of joy; I will sing to him in gratitude" (NET).

3. You discover a great truth about God when you realize He is your helper. Look at the following verses and record what you learn about the Lord's help. Personalize your observations like this: "God is my refuge and strength" (Psalm 46:1).

Deuteronomy 33:26

2 Samuel 8:13-14

2 Samuel 22:7,17-20

Psalm 37:39-40

Psalm 46:1

Psalm 54:4

ADORE GOD IN PRAYER

Turn to the prayer pages in the back of this book and devote one page to all the areas where you need God's help. Be sure to date each request. Then, when God answers you can give Him all the glory!

YIELD YOURSELF TO GOD

Meditate on these words by Charles Spurgeon as an encouragement to trust in the Lord in everything that comes your way:

> In seasons of severe trial, the Christian has nothing on earth that he can trust to, and is therefore compelled to cast himself on his God alone. When his vessel is on its beam-ends, and no human deliverance can avail, he must simply and entirely trust himself to the providence and care of God. Happy storm that wrecks a man on such a rock as this! O blessed hurricane that drives the soul to God and God alone! There is no getting at our God sometimes because of the multitude of our friends; but when a man is so poor, so friendless, so helpless that he has nowhere else to turn, he flies into his Father's arms, and is blessedly clasped therein! When he is burdened with troubles so pressing and so peculiar, that he cannot tell them to any but his God, he may be thankful for them; for he will learn more of his Lord then than at any other time. Oh, tempest-tossed believer, it is a happy trouble that drives thee to thy Father! Now that thou hast only thy God to trust to, see that thou puttest thy full confidence in him. Dishonour not thy Lord and Master by unworthy doubts and fears; but be strong in faith, giving glory to God. Show the world that thy God is worth ten thousand worlds to thee. Show rich men how rich thou art in thy poverty when the Lord God is thy helper. Show the strong man how strong thou art in thy weakness when underneath thee are the everlasting arms. Now is the time for feats of faith and valiant exploits. Be strong and very courageous, and the Lord thy God shall certainly, as surely as he built the heavens and the earth, glorify himself in thy weakness, and magnify his might in the midst of thy distress. The grandeur of the arch of heaven would be spoiled if the sky were supported by a single visible column, and your faith would lose its glory if it rested on anything discernible by the carnal eye. May the Holy Spirit give you to rest in Jesus.[10]

ENJOY HIS PRESENCE

What is the most important truth you learned today about trust and the help of the Lord?

REST IN HIS LOVE

"Behold, God is my helper; the LORD is the sustainer of my soul" (Psalm 54:4).

THE DECLARATION OF TRUST

Some trust in chariots and some in horses,
but we trust in the name of the LORD our God.
PSALM 20:7 NIV

PREPARE YOUR HEART

When you face difficult circumstances, do you complain about your plight, or do you champion the names of your God? Could you be called God's cheerleader or the world's complainer? Throughout Psalms, David confesses again and again what he knows about His God, what he has seen God do, and all God promises him. And you must do the same.

Charles Wesley wrote the beloved hymn "O for a Thousand Tongues to Sing" in honor of the one-year celebration of his conversion to Christ. Meditate on these words as a preparation of heart and ask the Lord to give you a thousand tongues to sing about all that you know of God and His names.

O for a thousand tongues to sing
My great Redeemer's praise,
The glories of my God and King,
The triumphs of His grace!

My gracious Master and my God,
Assist me to proclaim,
To spread through all the earth abroad
The honors of Thy name.

Jesus! the name that charms our fears,
That bids our sorrows cease;
'Tis music in the sinner's ears,
'Tis life, and health, and peace.

He breaks the power of canceled sin,
He sets the prisoner free;

His blood can make the foulest clean,
His blood availed for me.

Hear Him, ye deaf; His praise, ye dumb,
Your loosened tongues employ;
Ye blind, behold your Savior come,
And leap, ye lame, for joy.

READ AND STUDY GOD'S WORD

1. Begin your time in the Word of God today by reading through Psalm 20. What is most significant to you as you read this psalm?

2. Read Psalm 20 again and record every phrase or sentence by David that indicates trust in the Lord.

3. David declared, "Some trust in chariots and some in horses, but we trust in the name of the LORD our God" (Psalm 20:7 NIV). Why do you think a declaration of trust helps you trust in God more?

ADORE GOD IN PRAYER

Take some time today and thank the Lord for all you have learned about Him. Use a journal page in the back of this book to write out some declarations of trust in who He is and what He does.

YIELD YOURSELF TO GOD

God of the impossible,
Grant our heart's desire:
Faith for the impossible,
Love that cannot tire,

Hope that never faileth
Hope that shall inspire.[11]

AMY CARMICHAEL

ENJOY HIS PRESENCE

This week we have explored what it means to trust in His names. We have seen that the names of God are the foundation of our trust. We must *discover* His names and then *draw near* to His names. Then, we saw the great value of the prayer of trust, in which we call upon His names and even *declare* His names. We discovered that our trust is often tested in the heat of a trial. Therefore, in those dark times, we must *depend* on His names. The result of our dependence is deliverance and help in our time of trouble. Oh what praise will result when you see God at work in your life! You will then *delight* in His names.

As you think about your time in God's word, your prayer and devotion, and your meditation on different quotes and illustrations, what is the most important truth you have learned about trust this week?

REST IN HIS LOVE

"We will sing for joy over your victory, and in the name of our God we will set up our banners. May the LORD fulfill all your petitions" (Psalm 20:5).

DEVOTIONAL READING
BY ALAN REDPATH

What is your need today? Is it for pardon? "I have blotted out, as a thick cloud, thy transgressions" (Isaiah 44:22). Is it for peace? "My peace I give unto you: not as the world giveth…let not your heart be troubled" (John 14:27). Is it for guidance? "I will instruct thee and teach thee in the way which thou shalt go: I will guide thee with mine eye" (Psalm 32:8). Is it for holiness? "Be ye therefore perfect, even as your Father which is in heaven is perfect" (Matthew 5:48). Is it to be with Him in glory one day? "Father, I will that they also, whom thou hast given me, be with me where I am" (John 17:24). There is not a need of any one of our lives but is covered by a promise from the Word of God. He has put it into our hearts to ask because first of all it was in His heart to give. And when God has said "No" to the ambition of your life, to something that is very precious to you, He brings you close to His heart and shows you that every need of your soul is met by His promises. He wants to teach you, in the face of His negative answer, to learn to make your own every possible promise in the book. "Let us therefore come boldly unto the throne of grace, that we may obtain mercy, and find grace to help in time of need" (Hebrews 4:16).[12]

Take some time now to write about all that you have learned this week. How do these truths give you courage to trust in the Lord? What has been most significant to you? Close by writing a prayer to the Lord.

BEHOLD HIS BEAUTY
IN CREATION

It is evident a man may as well doubt whether there be a sun, when he sees its beams gilding the earth, as doubt whether there be a God, when he sees his works spread in the world.

STEPHEN CHARNOCK

BEHOLD YOUR GOD

In the beginning, God created the heavens and the earth.

GENESIS 1:1

PREPARE YOUR HEART

Before time, there was only eternity, with no beginning and no end. Before time existed, before anything existed, God was self-existent and uncreated. We can say such things about God only because He has told us—He has revealed Himself to us. In the Bible, His Word, the very first sentence reads, "In the beginning God created the heavens and the earth." This one sentence settles many questions in life. Yes, there is a God. And yes, He has made Himself known. And yes, He is the Designer behind the grand design. Knowing God exists changes everything about how you live life. You cannot rightfully ignore Him. He exists, and He has spoken. We have His written Word in the Bible. This is such incredibly happy news for you. Why? Because now you can launch out on the most amazing adventure of discovery—the great discovery of God.

As you begin your quiet time today, ask God to speak to you in His Word and reveal Himself to you.

READ AND STUDY GOD'S WORD

1. The fact that God has revealed Himself to us is a profound truth for you to think about. Look at the following verses and record what you learn about God making Himself known to you:

Deuteronomy 29:29

1 Samuel 2:27

Psalm 19:1-2

Psalm 98:2

Daniel 2:20-23

Romans 1:18-20

2. God's revelation of Himself to men and women occurs over time. In other words, He did not tell us all at once everything He wanted to reveal. Instead, He chose a progression of revelation to different men and women in different historical circumstances. Over the course of this quiet time experience, we will look at the life situations of some of these men and women and enter into their life stories to behold the beauty of the Lord as He revealed Himself to them. Summarize in two or three sentences what you have learned about God making Himself known to us.

3. Read Genesis 1:1 and write it out word for word in the space provided.

4. The word for "God" in Genesis 1:1 is the first name God gives to us. The Hebrew for "God" is *Elohim* and refers to the One true God, with the root *El* meaning "mighty one, strength."[1] The plural form of this noun points to God as the Triune God. *Elohim* is used 35 times in the first two chapters of Genesis in connection with His power in creation. Think about the existence of God, His revelation to you, and the fact that He begins the Bible with this name.

Why is knowing that God exists and that He is the author of creation important to you? How does such knowledge make a difference in your own life?

ADORE GOD IN PRAYER

My soul wakes early and turns to you, O God, for the light. Your light is better than life; therefore, my lips shall praise you. Take my hand in yours, and make the crooked places straight and the rough places plain, that your name may be glorified in my daily walk and conversation.[2]

F.B. MEYER

YIELD YOURSELF TO GOD

How could this great heap be brought into being, unless a God had framed it? Every plant, every atom, as well as every star, at the first meeting, whispers this in our ears, *I have a Creator; I am witness to a Deity…* Who beholds garments, ships, or houses, but understands there was a weaver, a carpenter, and architect? Who can cast his eyes about the world, but must think of that power that formed it, and that the goodness which appears in the formation of it hath a perfect residence in some being? Those things that are good must flow from something perfectly good: that which is chief in any kind is the cause of all of that kind. Fire which is most hot, is the cause of all things which are hot. There is some being, therefore, which is the cause of all that perfection which is in the creature; and this is God…

God hath given us sense to behold the objects in the world, and understanding to reason His existence from them. The understanding cannot conceive a thing to have made itself; that is against all reason. As they are made, they speak out a Maker, and cannot be a trick of chance, since they are made with such an immense wisdom, that is too big for the grasp of human understanding.[3]

STEPHEN CHARNOCK

ENJOY HIS PRESENCE

What a joy that God has revealed Himself! He has given many names for Himself and shown His ways and works in the lives of different men and women in the Bible. The Lord takes you on a journey of discovery, revealing Himself to you as you draw near to Him. He does not show you everything there is to know all at once. That is why your relationship with Him is such an ongoing joy—an adventure. You never know what He is going to show you about Himself next.

And so, dear friend, as we continue on in this quiet time experience of trusting in the names of God, get ready to behold your God. As you close your time with the Lord today, write out your most significant insight. Then thank the Lord for all He is showing you and for revealing Himself to you.

REST IN HIS LOVE

"It is He who reveals the profound and hidden things; He knows what is in the darkness, and the light dwells with Him" (Daniel 2:22).

THE DAY GOD PAINTED THE SKY

Then God said, "Let there be light"; and there was light.

GENESIS 1:3

PREPARE YOUR HEART

All of heaven must have watched in wonder as the Triune God—Elohim, the Father, Son, and Holy Spirit—in perfect harmony wove a beautiful creation. God spoke, and light came into existence. God separated the light from the darkness. What does that mean? He knows. God named the light and the darkness. Day and night came into being. God spoke again and made the heavens. He painted the sky without moving a hand—the power of His Word was enough to fling stars into galaxy upon galaxy with myriads upon myriads of planets in perfect orbit according to His design. He commanded dry land to appear, and the earth came into existence. He spoke, and vegetation sprouted and grew. He spoke again and again and again, creating all that was in His mind to create. And He saw it all and called it good—He who is perfect made everything perfectly.

Begin your time with the Lord today by reading Psalm 19:1-6 and writing out your most significant insight from these words. Ask God to quiet your heart so you can hear Him speak. Be willing, dear friend, to slow down and think great thoughts about God.

READ AND STUDY GOD'S WORD

1. Take some time now and read Genesis 1. Use one-word descriptions to write out everything that the text says God has created.

2. God spoke the earth and the universe into existence. Describe how powerful His Word must be.

3. How does knowing the power of His Word motivate you to open your Bible each day to hear what He has to say to you?

ADORE GOD IN PRAYER

Pray the words of Psalm 104:24-25,31,33-34 today:

> O LORD, how many are Your works!
> In wisdom You have made them all;
> The earth is full of Your possessions.
> There is the sea, great and broad,
> In which are swarms without number,
> Animals both small and great…
> Let the glory of the LORD endure forever;
> Let the LORD be glad in His works…
> I will sing to the LORD as long as I live;
> I will sing praise to my God while I have my being.
> Let my meditation be pleasing to Him;
> As for me, I shall be glad in the LORD.

YIELD YOURSELF TO GOD

Meditate on these words by Henry Law from his little treasure on Psalms, *Daily Prayer and Praise:*

> Debased and senseless is the mind which creation's wonders fail to touch. Survey the canopy above our heads. It is magnificent in all which constitutes beauty and splendour in perfection. From morn to night light strides along its azure path, illumining the world. When evening's shades prevail, the stars hang out their

countless lamps, and stud with spangles the brilliant concave. We marvel; we admire. We trace the great Creator's skill and reverently adore. It must be a mighty mind which planned this exquisite machinery. It must be mighty power which framed these glowing orbs, and gave them their appointed courses. They could not will their own formation. They could not deck themselves with brightness. It must, too, be gracious benevolence which arranged such lovely helps and solace for us. On all the heavens God's glory is inscribed. The skies in all their parts show what His hands have wrought. The record never ceases. Day follows day, repeating the instruction. Night succeeds to night, telling the great Creator's praise.[4]

Reflect on these words by Gypsy Smith:

Listen—the fingers that weaved the rainbow into a scarf and wrapped it around the shoulders of the dying storm, the fingers that painted the lily-bell and threw out the planets, the fingers that were dipped in the mighty sea of eternity and shook out on this old planet, making the ocean to drop and the rivers to stream—the same fingers can take hold on these tangled lives and can make them whole again.[5]

ENJOY HIS PRESENCE

What is your most significant insight from your time with the Lord today? Close by writing a prayer to Him, expressing all that is on your heart.

REST IN HIS LOVE

"The heavens are telling of the glory of God; and their expanse is declaring the work of His hands" (Psalm 19:1).

THE DAY GOD SCULPTED A MAN

Then the LORD God formed man of dust from the ground,
and breathed into his nostrils the breath of life;
and man became a living being.
GENESIS 2:7

PREPARE YOUR HEART

The magnificent act of painting the sky with stars and planets was miniscule compared to what God was about to do. Creating the heavens, the earth, night and day, vegetation of every kind, living creatures in the waters, and birds in the sky took five days. Elohim spoke everything in those five days into existence. Now, on the sixth day, God—the Father, the Son, and the Holy Spirit—was going to do something new, unparalleled, and personal.

Here we see a new combination of names for God: *Yahweh Elohim.* You will see the meaning of *Yahweh* in more detail in week 5, but *Yahweh* is the personal covenant memorial name of God, used as God moves near to man, desiring to be his God in an intimate relationship. Here you see a personal, relational God leaning down from heaven to earth and sculpting a living being, a man, created in His own image. Then, God breathed life into man, the one He had formed from the dust of the ground. God even planted a garden, a perfect and beautiful environment, and placed man in the garden. Do you see the personal touch of Yahweh Elohim, your personal God, in creation? Can you let yourself be amazed again by the intricate design of man—the body, personality, intellect, soul, and spirit? Draw near to God today and ask Him to open your mind to meditate on and grasp in a new and deeper way how majestic He is.

READ AND STUDY GOD'S WORD

1. Read Genesis 1:26-31 and 2:5-8,15-25 and record everything you learn about the creation of man and woman.

2. Read Psalm 139:13-16 and write out everything you learn about how God created you.

3. Psalm 104:24 offers praise to the Lord for all His creation. The psalmist says, "O Lord, how many are Your works! In wisdom You have made them all." In every magnificent work of God, including the creation of men and women, we see God's wisdom. The Hebrew word for "wisdom" is *hokmah* and means "skill, experience, shrewdness." Read Proverbs 8:12-31, a profound passage of Scripture on the wisdom of God, and record what is most significant to you about God's wisdom. (The pronouns *me* and *I* in this passage refer to God's wisdom.)

ADORE GOD IN PRAYER

Pray the words of Psalm 145:1-6 today:

> I will extol You, my God, O King,
> And I will bless Your name forever and ever.
> Every day I will bless You,
> And I will praise Your name forever and ever.
> Great is the Lord, and highly to be praised,
> And His greatness is unsearchable.
> One generation shall praise Your works to another,
> And shall declare Your mighty acts.
> On the glorious splendor of Your majesty
> And on Your wonderful works, I will meditate.
> Men shall speak of the power of Your awesome acts,
> And I will tell of Your greatness.

YIELD YOURSELF TO GOD

Meditate on these words by Larry Richards:

"Let Us," God says, "make man in Our image, in Our likeness." And the text continues, "So God created man in His own image, in the image of God He created him; male and female He created them." The two Hebrew words used here to define the human essence are *selem* meaning "image" or "representation," and *demut,* which implies comparison. When linked they make a decisive theological statement. The essence of human nature can only be understood by comparison with God Himself. We can never understand man by referring back to some supposed emergence from prehistoric beasts. In a totally unique creative act, God gave Adam not only physical life but also personhood—his own capacity to think, to feel, to evaluate, to love, to choose, as a self-aware individual.

The Genesis account itself emphasizes human uniqueness. All other aspects of Creation were called into being by God's spoken word. Yet for man God stooped to personally fashion a physical body, and then gently, lovingly infused that body with life. In order that there should be no mistaking God's intent, God fashioned Eve from one of Adam's ribs. Genesis is clear. Adam and Eve share the same substance. They participate alike in the image and likeness given to beings alone.

This account does more than explain man's origins. It has the power to shape our most basic attitudes toward ourselves and others.

Consider. If I am made in the image of God, then I must have worth and value as an individual. It's irrelevant to compare myself with others if my essential being can be understood by comparison with God! Knowing God made me in His image, I learn to love and to value myself.

Have you ever noticed how we handle things we value? We wear the new watch or pin proudly. When we lay it aside, we do so carefully, putting it in a drawer where it won't be damaged or harmed. If you and I grasp the value of being created in God's image and likeness, we will come to appreciate ourselves too. We'll refuse to be degraded by others, and we will reject temptations that would harm us physically or spiritually. Because we bear the image and likeness of the Creator, we are too significant to mar.

Consider. If others are made in the image and likeness of God, they must have worth and value as individuals, whatever weaknesses they display. When I understand that every human being shares the image-likeness of God, I will treat others with respect. I learn to overlook failures and to communicate love. I realize that the existence of God's image-likeness, however distorted by sin, means that the other person can respond, as I have, to the love of God displayed in Jesus Christ. So I reach out to him or her in love.[6]

ENJOY HIS PRESENCE

What is your most significant insight from your time with the Lord today? What have you learned that will help you trust Him more? Thank the Lord for all He is showing you.

REST IN HIS LOVE

"I will give thanks to You, for I am fearfully and wonderfully made; wonderful are Your works, and my soul knows it very well" (Psalm 139:14).

THE DAY GOD ANSWERED JOB

Then the LORD answered Job out of the whirlwind...
Where were you when I laid the foundations of the earth?

JOB 38:1,4

PREPARE YOUR HEART

When does the work and power of Elohim mean the most to you? Most likely, it's when you are suffering. In the heat of trouble, especially the fiery trial, no one seems to have the power to help. And often, there is nothing you can do. But when you calculate the creative power and might of Elohim into your trouble, you can trust Him for something outside the realm of your own thinking, for He can create something out of nothing. This is your hope today, dear friend. Turn your eyes away from the trouble and on to your God, Elohim, Creator of the universe and Creator of you.

READ AND STUDY GOD'S WORD

1. Read Psalm 34:15-18 and write out everything you learn about the Lord's work on behalf of those who are suffering and in pain.

2. Probably very few have suffered the multitude of troubles all at once that Job experienced. In fact, whenever you think through the difficult life experiences of different men and women in the Bible, Job most likely comes to your mind. Job was, according to the Bible, "blameless, upright, fearing God and turning away from evil" (Job 1:1). For one brief moment, we are granted a glimpse into an event in the very presence of God: Satan is granted permission to test Job. In

one day, Job lost all his children, all his possessions, his home…everything except his wife (see Job 1:2-22). We are told in Scripture that "through all this Job did not sin nor did he blame God." Then Job suffers physical adversity, and his wife even tells him he should curse God. Job still did not sin. Throughout the chapters of Job we find a wrestling and reasoning about suffering. Finally, God speaks to Job (Job 38–41). Read Job 38:1-18,34-38 and write what is most significant to you about God and what He can do.

3. Read Job 42:1-5 and describe how Job responded to God's revelation of Himself.

4. Don't you find it interesting that one of God's greatest revelations of Himself came to someone who suffered the most? Take heart, dear friend, if you are suffering. In the heat of your trial, when you draw near to God, trusting Him, you are going to see your God anew. As a result, you will become more intimate with Him.

Read Job 42:10 and note the final outcome for Job. Then read James 5:11 and write what you learn about Job and what you learn about God.

ADORE GOD IN PRAYER

Lift me up, by your strong arm, above the mists and darkness of the valley, to stand and walk with you on the high level of your presence and glory.[7]

F.B. MEYER

YIELD YOURSELF TO GOD

Meditate on these words by Charles Spurgeon:

"This poor man cried out, and the LORD heard him" (Ps. 34:6). The man was alone, and the only one who heard him was the Lord. Yes, the Lord, Jehovah of Hosts, the All-glorious, heard his prayer. God stooped from His eternal glory and gave attention to this cry. Never think that a praying heart pleads to a deaf God. Never imagine that God is so far removed that He fails to notice our needs. God hears prayer and grants His children's desires and requests…

Amid all the innumerable actions of divine power, the Lord never ceases to listen to the cries of those who seek His face. This verse is always true, "The righteous cry, and the LORD heareth, and delivereth them out of all their troubles" (Ps. 34:17). What a glorious fact! Truly marvelous! This is still Jehovah's special title: the God who hears prayer. We often come from the throne of grace as certain that God heard us as we were sure that we had prayed. The abounding answers to our supplications are proof positive that prayer climbs above the regions of earth and time and touches God and His infinity. Yes, it is still true, the Lord will hear your prayer.[8]

ENJOY HIS PRESENCE

What have you learned today that will help you trust Elohim in a time of trouble?

REST IN HIS LOVE

"The LORD is near to the brokenhearted and saves those who are crushed in spirit" (Psalm 34:18).

TRUSTING IN ELOHIM

Heed the sound of my cry for help, my King and my God, for to You I pray.
PSALM 5:2

PREPARE YOUR HEART

Samuel Rutherford, Scottish theologian, pastor, and author, lived in the 1600s. He faithfully ministered to a small congregation, sometimes experiencing very little fruit in ministry. And yet he continually drew near to God in communion with Him and faithfully studied the Bible. His book on grace was so radical in its day that he was exiled to Aberdeen and warned never to preach in Scotland again. For two years he was known as the "banished minister." During those years in exile he wrote what later became his greatest work, *The Letters of Samuel Rutherford.* Spurgeon often read Rutherford's letters and derived much blessing from them. These precious, encouraging letters, written to hundreds of people, are selfless, Scripture-filled devotionals on life with the Lord. In one letter he wrote this:

> I am most ready at the good pleasure of my Lord, in the strength of His grace, for anything He will be pleased to call me to…If my Lord will take honor of the like of me, how glad and joyful will my soul be. Let Christ come out with me to a hotter battle than this, and I will fear no flesh. I know that my Master shall win the day, and that He has taken the order of my suffering into His own hand.[9]

His words to his distant flock of parishioners point to his great help and resource in his time of trouble—the Lord Himself.

Who do you run to for help in life? When you begin to grasp the power of Elohim, you will cry out to Him in prayer. David cried out to Elohim when he said, "Heed the sound of my cry for help, my King and my God, for to You I pray" (Psalm 5:2). Note that David called Him "my God," or "my Elohim." Is God personal to you? Maybe you are wondering if calling Him "my God" is too presumptuous. Dear friend, understand that Elohim Himself desires to be *your* God, *your* Elohim. He said to the people of Israel in Exodus 6:7, "I will take you for My people, and I will be your God; and you shall know that I am the LORD your God." When you realize He is *your* God and you draw near to His heart, you will run to Him in your deepest needs.

Begin your quiet time today reading Psalm 5:1-3 and writing out what you learn about prayer. Ask God to speak to you as you draw near to Him.

READ AND STUDY GOD'S WORD

1. This week you have had the opportunity to glimpse into the many facets of Elohim. *Elohim* is a primary name for God and occurs more than 2000 times in the Bible. Look at the following verses and record what you learn about your God, your Elohim:

Genesis 45:4-8

Deuteronomy 3:22

Psalm 7:9-11

Psalm 18:28-29

Psalm 46:10

Psalm 47:6-9

2. What is your most significant insight about God, your Elohim, from the Word today?

ADORE GOD IN PRAYER

Turn to the prayer pages in the back of this book and write out any new requests to take to Elohim today. How does knowing Elohim give you confidence to call out to Him? Thank Him for what He is showing you about Himself.

YIELD YOURSELF TO GOD

Because we are the handiwork of God, it follows that all our problems and their solutions are theological. Some knowledge of what kind of God it is that operates the universe is indispensable to a sound philosophy of life and a sane outlook on the world scene…We can never know who or what we are till we know at least something of what God is. For this reason the self-existence of God is not a wisp of dry doctrine, academic and remote; it is in fact as near as our breath and as practical as the latest surgical technique…For reasons known only to Himself, God honored man above all other beings by creating him in His own image…Man is a created being, a derived and contingent self, who of himself possesses nothing but is dependent each moment for his existence upon the One who created him after His own likeness. The fact of God is necessary to the fact of man.[10]

A.W. TOZER

ENJOY HIS PRESENCE

Think about all you have learned of Elohim this week. What is your favorite truth about Elohim? How will knowing Elohim make a difference in how you live your life?

REST IN HIS LOVE

"Cease striving and know that I am God" (Psalm 46:10).

DEVOTIONAL READING
BY MATTHEW HENRY

In the visible world it is easy to observe, [1.] Great variety, several sorts of beings vastly differing in their nature and constitution from each other. *Lord, how manifold are thy works,* and all good! [2.] Great beauty. The azure sky and verdant earth are charming to the eye of the curious spectator, much more the ornaments of both. How transcendent then must the beauty of the Creator be! [3.] Great exactness and accuracy. To those that, with the help of microscopes, narrowly look into the works of nature, they appear far more fine than any of the works of art. [4.] Great power. It is not a lump of dead and inactive matter, but there is virtue, more or less, in every creature: the earth itself has a magnetic power. [5.] Great order, a mutual dependence of beings, an exact harmony of motions, and an admirable chain and connection of causes. [6.] Great mystery. There are phenomena in nature which cannot be solved, secrets which cannot be fathomed nor accounted for. But from what we see of heaven and earth we may easily enough infer the eternal power and Godhead of the great Creator, and may furnish ourselves with abundant matter for his praises. And let our make and place, as men, remind us of our duty as Christians, which is always to keep heaven in our eye and the earth under our feet.[11]

Take some time now to write about all that you have learned this week. What has been most significant to you? Close by writing a prayer to the Lord.

BEHOLD HIS BEAUTY
WITH THE FRIEND
OF GOD

When we give up ourselves in heart, mind, and will to God, He becomes ours to possess and enjoy! When we cease to be our own, we become His. When we lose ourselves in Him, we find ourselves.

DWIGHT HERVEY SMALL

THE DAY GOD MADE A FRIEND

Abraham believed God, and it was credited to him as righteousness, and he was called God's friend.

JAMES 2:23 NIV

PREPARE YOUR HEART

What is the greatest claim to fame anyone can have? Some people have built great houses, achieved high positions of power, or amassed much wealth. But one of the greatest claims to fame recorded in the Bible is that of Abraham. He was God's friend. Can you imagine what it would mean to experience such intimacy with your God that He calls you His friend? Such was the relationship between God and Abraham. This week we will explore in greater detail the friendship between God and Abraham. Draw near to God now and ask Him for that same kind of intimate relationship—friendship with Him.

READ AND STUDY GOD'S WORD

1. Abraham is a towering personality in the Bible and is repeatedly mentioned in both the Old and New Testaments. Who was Abraham? His story begins in Genesis on the day God met him and made great promises to him. Read Genesis 11:26–12:5 and record everything you learn about Abraham. (Until Genesis 17 he is called Abram.)

2. Read Genesis 12:1-5 again. Note that God not only makes great promises to Abraham but also asks Abraham to make a huge change in his life. What was God asking Abraham to do, and how did Abraham respond to God's request?

3. When God asked Abraham to leave his home, God revealed His name *Adonai,* showing that He was Abraham's Lord, Master, and Owner. *Adonai* is always translated "Lord" (with a capital *L* and subsequent lowercase letters). *Adonai* is the one who directs your decisions, guides your actions, and commands your obedience. Read Genesis 15:1-2 and record your most significant insight about God's promise (in verse 1) and Abraham's question (in verse 2). Think about how the knowledge that God is your Lord, Master, and Owner impacts your trust in Him to fulfill His great promises even when your situation looks hopeless.

4. The New Testament offers insight into the life of Abraham and what made him such a hero of the faith. Read Hebrews 11:8-16 and record your most significant insight about Abraham.

5. Abraham became known as God's friend. Look at the following verses and take note about what is said regarding the relationship of Abraham with his God.

2 Chronicles 20:7

Isaiah 41:8

James 2:23

6. Think about all you have learned today about Abraham. What qualities do you think made him so different from the average man or woman? Why does the Bible speak of him with such great respect? Why was he God's friend? Write your insights in the space provided.

ADORE GOD IN PRAYER

Talk with the Lord today about your own relationship with Him. How intimate are you with the Lord? Are you His friend? Use a journal page at the back of this book to write a prayer, expressing all that is on your heart.

YIELD YOURSELF TO GOD

Meditate on these words by Dwight Hervey Small about Abraham:

> Ur was a place where a young man might find everything, yet God simply said to Abraham, "Leave it. Go where I will lead you." Promptly Abraham obeyed and went out, leaving behind all the privileges of the city lifestyle. He burned his bridges, trusting God to manage his affairs. How foolish this must have seemed to his faithless friends and family…
>
> Like Abraham, we are called to regard ourselves as mere sojourners in this world, not so much because earth is fleeting and its values are transient, but because our true affinities are with the unseen and the eternal. However, as Tersteegen says, "Our nature fights against the thought of venturing forth we know not where." We often take on the attitude that earth is our permanent home. But Abraham was willing to wander because God called him to do so; he was separated from home and kin in order to be separated to God…
>
> Abraham's departure from Ur marked the beginning of a great epoch in faith's response to God. Had he refused to obey, he would have sunk into the obscurity of an unknown Mesopotamian grave, forever lost to all future ages. But Abraham did obey, and in that decisive act he laid the foundation for a noble life of growing faith and deepening love. He became a hero of faith for us.[1]

ENJOY HIS PRESENCE

Every man or woman of God must one day, like Abraham, launch out on God's promises, not knowing where he or she is going. God will ask you to step out and trust Him as your Lord and Master. When you say yes, your friendship with God will grow deeper. Your trust in God as your Adonai brings great delight to His heart. You can see that when Abraham packed up his bags, gathered together his family, and chose to live in tents, his actions indicated his trust in God's promise to him. F.B. Meyer says that it was his "unquestioning obedience that endeared him to God."[2]

What is God asking of you today? What will it take for you to trust Adonai in your own life? Will you have the absolute and unquestioning obedience of an Abraham? Dear friend, even opening your Bible and drawing near to God in quiet time is an indication of your trust in Him. Are you committed to daily quiet time with God? Perhaps God has given you an idea for serving Him, but you have been resisting the opportunity. Take some time now to write out your thoughts in the space provided. Then ask God to give you a deeper trust in Him and a more intimate friendship with Him.

Rest in His Love

"By faith Abraham, when he was called, obeyed by going out to a place which he was to receive for an inheritance; and he went out, not knowing where he was going" (Hebrews 11:8).

CALLING ON THE NAME OF THE LORD

There he built an altar to the LORD and called upon the name of the LORD.
GENESIS 12:8

PREPARE YOUR HEART

When God called Abraham to go to an unknown land, He took His friend on an incredible journey. Abraham left his home and arrived at the land of Canaan. Now what? God appeared to Abraham and promised him again, "To your descendants I will give this land" (Genesis 12:7). What a promise to one who had no children and was living in a tent. And yet the one who made the promise was God. The identity of the promise-giver changes everything. Abraham knew God would keep His word. How did Abraham respond? He "built an altar to the LORD and called upon the name of the LORD" (Genesis 12:8).

Men and women of God who desire to grow in their relationship with their Lord eventually discover the secret of Abraham and find a special place where they can pray and express their trust in God and His promises of who He is, what He does, and what He says. Today you will discover more about calling on the name of the Lord.

READ AND STUDY GOD'S WORD

1. If you've ever read through the Bible in a year, you know the wonder and amazement of observing the unfolding of God's plan, beginning with Genesis, moving through Exodus, and continuing on throughout the entire Bible. One interesting observation you may make has to do with the point in time when people began calling on the name of the Lord. After Abel was killed by Cain, Adam and Eve had another son named Seth. We are told in Genesis 4:26 that after Seth had a son named Enosh, "people began to call on the name of the LORD."

This statement is so significant, setting an example for us to follow. What does it mean to call on His name? The Hebrew word translated "call" is *qara,* "to declare, summon, cry out." The context of Genesis 4 includes the proud self-reliance of Lamech. Then we are introduced to Seth and Enosh, ushering in a new era when people begin to depend on God and worship Him. Here the name translated LORD is *Yahweh (YHVH)*—the personal, covenant, memorial name of God. The Patriarchs knew God as Yahweh, but we learn much more about this name when God revealed Himself to Moses and told Moses about His plan to deliver His people from the oppression of the Egyptians. (We will study this in more detail in week 5.)

Look at the following verses and record what you learn about calling on the name of the Lord:

Genesis 4:26

Genesis 12:8

Genesis 26:24-25

1 Kings 18:22-24

1 Chronicles 16:7-8

Psalm 116:16-19

Joel 2:32

Zephaniah 3:9

1 Corinthians 1:1-3

2. Summarize in two or three sentences what you have learned about calling on the name of the Lord and what it means to call on His name.

ADORE GOD IN PRAYER

Take some time now to call on the name of the Lord and place your dependence on Him in every area of your life.

YIELD YOURSELF TO GOD

Paul has given you a wonderful promise in Philippians 4:6-7: "Be anxious for nothing, but in everything by prayer and supplication with thanksgiving let your requests be made known to God. And the peace of God, which surpasses all comprehension, will guard your hearts and your minds in Christ Jesus." These words of Paul instruct believers how to call on God's names in the heat of stress and trial.

Meditate on these words by F.B. Meyer:

> We must ever practice the presence of our Lord—he is always at hand. We must turn over all causes of anxiety to the Father's infinite care and leave them with him. We must thank him for the past and count on him for the future. While we pray, God's peace will descend to stand as sentry at our heart's door.[3]

ENJOY HIS PRESENCE

Abraham provides an example for us as he engages in one practice that is necessary for anyone who would be a friend of God. He was a man of prayer. He had a habit of calling on the name of the Lord along the path of his journey. He responded to the words of God by building an altar, calling on God's name, and worshipping Him. Friend, have you set aside a quiet place and formed the habit of calling on God's names and worshipping Him? What have you learned that will help you become practiced in prayer to your Lord? How important do you think it is to know the names of God and call on Him by name? Close your time with the Lord today by writing a prayer to Him, expressing all that is on your heart.

REST IN HIS LOVE

"Don't worry about anything; instead, pray about everything. Tell God what you need, and thank him for all he has done. Then you will experience God's peace, which exceeds anything we can understand. His peace will guard your hearts and minds as you live in Christ Jesus" (Philippians 4:6-7 NLT).

EL SHADDAI—A GREAT GOD FOR A GREAT PROMISE

I am God Almighty; walk before Me, and be blameless.

GENESIS 17:1

PREPARE YOUR HEART

God was about to accomplish the impossible in the life of His friend Abraham. But before He worked His miracles for both Abraham and Sarah, He gave them promises about what He was going to do. These were the "I wills" from God to Abraham, promises of who He is, what He does, and what He says.

Why does God give promises? He wants you to live by faith, not by sight (2 Corinthians 5:7). Therefore, God promises, and now the challenge is on: Will you take Him at His word? Will you believe God for what He has promised? God not only gives great promises but also reveals His own greatness to you—and you will discover He is more than enough for all He promises to do. And so it was with Abraham. God revealed to Abraham and Sarah that He was more than enough for the absolutely incredible promises He was making in their lives. You see, when you know the names of God, you will trust in Him (Psalm 9:10). Abraham trusted and became a great hero of the faith. And so will you as you learn to trust God in the face of your impossible situations. Ask God to grow your trust in Him so that you will be a hero of the faith.

READ AND STUDY GOD'S WORD

1. Imagine you are in Abraham's shoes. You're 99 years old with no children and no real home to call your own. God appears to you and says He is going to make you the father of many nations and give you abundant land for an everlasting possession. How would you respond? Read Genesis 17:1-8 and record all the promises God made to Abraham, including who He is, what He will do, and what He says.

Who He is:

What He will do:

What He says:

2. Read Genesis 17:15-19. What was Abraham's response? Why was this promise so seemingly impossible?

3. God revealed Himself as God Almighty to Abraham. The words translated "God Almighty" are *El Shaddai* and reveal that God nourishes, supplies, and satisfies. He has all power and is all-sufficient—more than enough for whatever your life requires. God made spectacular promises to Abraham. But then He showed Abraham that He was enough for those promises, yes, even more than enough, for He is God Almighty, El Shaddai, the all-sufficient one. Look at the following verses and record what you learn about God Almighty, El Shaddai.

Genesis 28:1-5

Genesis 35:9-15 (see also Genesis 48:3)

Psalm 91:1

Ezekiel 1:24

Ezekiel 10:4-5

4. What El Shaddai promises, He will do. The Lord said to Abraham, "Is anything too difficult for the LORD? At the appointed time I will return to you, at this time next year, and Sarah will have a son" (Genesis 18:14). Now just imagine what this time in Abraham's life must have really been like. At the ages of 100 and 99 and Abraham and Sarah were about to begin a whole new phase of their lives. Read Genesis 21:1-8 and write your insights about how El Shaddai fulfilled His promise.

ADORE GOD IN PRAYER

Are you in a situation that requires more power and resources than you can produce on your own? Run to El Shaddai and thank Him that He is God Almighty, the all-sufficient one. Use a prayer page in the back of this book to list all your needs requiring the supply and sufficiency of El Shaddai. Ask Him to meet your needs as only He can. Be sure to record how He answers your prayers in the days to come.

YIELD YOURSELF TO GOD

Meditate on these words by A.W. Tozer:

> If there is a desire in your heart for more of God's blessing in your life, turn your attention to the details of Abraham's encounters with God. You will find yourself back at the center, at the beating heart of living religions…Abraham had no Bible and no hymnal. He had no church and no godly religious traditions for guidance. He could not turn to a minister or an evangelist for spiritual help. Abraham had only his own empty, hungry heart. That and the manifestation of the God who reveals Himself to men and women who desire to find Him and know Him!…
>
> Think about the reality of Abraham's experience. Abraham was consciously aware of God, His presence and His revelation. He was aware that the living God had stepped over the threshold into personal encounter with a man who found the desire within himself to know God, to believe God and to live for God. See the effect of this encounter on Abraham. He was prepared to pay any price for the privilege of knowing God. For certain he recognized the lofty, holy character of the Creator and Revealer God…

Yes, Abraham was lying face down in humility and reverence, overcome with awe in this encounter with God. He knew that he was surrounded by the world's greatest mystery. The presence of this One who fills all things was pressing in upon him, rising above him, defeating him, taking away his natural self-confidence. God was overwhelming him and yet inviting and calling him, pleading with him and promising him a great future as a friend of God.[4]

ENJOY HIS PRESENCE

Two of the magnificent New Testament promises of the all-sufficiency of God are in 2 Corinthians: "And God is able to make all grace abound to you, so that always having all sufficiency in everything, you may have an abundance for every good deed" (9:8), and "My grace is sufficient for you, for power is perfected in weakness" (12:9). Think about how you need "an abundance for every good deed" and how you need His power perfected in your weakness today. Close by using a journal page to write a prayer to your Lord, expressing all that is on your heart today.

REST IN HIS LOVE

"And God is able to make all grace abound to you, so that always having all sufficiency in everything, you may have an abundance for every good deed" (2 Corinthians 9:8).

EL OLAM—AN ETERNAL GOD FOR AN ETERNAL FRIEND

Abraham planted a tamarisk tree at Beersheba, and there he called on the name of the LORD, the Everlasting God.

GENESIS 21:33

PREPARE YOUR HEART

What an amazing experience Abraham must have had, walking with God as his friend. Abraham has much to teach us and is included in the hall of fame of faith in Hebrews 11. As you read through the chapters of Genesis, you begin to see the progressive nature of the revelation of God to His friend Abraham. He had shown Himself as Elohim (the Creator), El Elyon (the sovereign one), Adonai (the Lord), El Shaddai (God Almighty), and Yahweh Jireh (the provider). Abraham responded with faith and learned what it meant to truly trust in his God. He was a champion of TRUST (Total Reliance Under Stress and Trial). And why could he trust day by day in the midst of his circumstances? He knew who God was and relied on God to be faithful and true. As you begin your quiet time today, ask God to quiet your heart and help you have a faith and trust like Abraham's.

READ AND STUDY GOD'S WORD

Abraham, God's friend, had walked with God for many years. He experienced the faithfulness of God as he saw the birth of his son Isaac. After making a treaty with Abimelech, he planted a tamarisk tree and called on the Lord with a new name, *El Olam*—Eternal God. The Hebrew word *olam* means "everlasting" and includes the immutability, the unchangeableness of God. When you think of El Olam, think of the stability of God that endures forever. Everything else may change, but God never changes. Oh, what a comfort this must have been to Abraham. To know God never changes is to have rock-solid security in the midst of ever-changing circumstances and relationships. Charles Wesley wrote, "And all things as they change proclaim the Lord eternally the same." There is one relationship you can always count on—your friendship with God.

1. Read Genesis 21:22-34 and record what you see about Abraham's relationship with God.

2. Think about the following verses and record what you learn about the eternal nature of God:

Deuteronomy 33:27

Psalm 90:2

Psalm 106:1

Psalm 117:2

Psalm 135:13

Isaiah 40:28

3. The wonderful truth is that you, like Abraham, are given the opportunity for friendship with your eternal God. Jesus said, "I have called you friends" (John 15:15). The Greek word

translated "friends" is *philos* and refers to a close personal friend and confidant. Read John 15:12-17 and describe what you learn about friendship with Jesus.

4. Just think, Jesus calls you His friend! What a privileged position you enjoy! Because of this friendship, Jesus has chosen to share God's words with you. He says, "I have called you friends, for all things that I have heard from My Father I have made known to you" (John 15:15). When you think about it, His words here about friendship give you a new perspective of the Bible. Is He not, in fact, sharing His heart with you in His Word when you open the pages of your Bible and read what He says? When you realize how God is opening up Himself to you in His Word, you cannot help but be motivated to draw near, read and think about what He is saying, and take seriously what He is confiding to you as He shares His heart in His Word. Think about how He revealed His heart to His friend Abraham when He described what He was going to do in Sodom and Gomorrah. As you think about these truths, write out what it means to you to have the opportunity to enjoy a friendship with the Lord.

ADORE GOD IN PRAYER

Talk with El Olam, your Everlasting God, and lay all your burdens and desires in His eternal and able hands. Cast all your anxiety on Him, "because He cares for you" (1 Peter 5:7).

YIELD YOURSELF TO GOD

Meditate on these thoughts about the eternity of God by Stephen Charnock and think about how God's eternal nature affects your friendship with Him:

> His duration is as endless as his essence is boundless: he always was and always will be, and will no more have an end than he had a beginning; and this is an excellency belonging to the Supreme Being. As his essence comprehends all beings, and exceeds them, and his immensity surmounts all places; so his eternity comprehends all times, all durations, and infinitely excels them...

As God is, so will the eternity of him be, without succession, without division; the fulness of joy will be always present; without past to be thought of with regret for being gone; without future to be expected with tormenting desires. When we enjoy God, we enjoy him in his eternity without any flux; an entire possession of all together, without the passing away of pleasures that may be wished to return, or expectation of future joys which might be desired to hasten. Time is fluid, but eternity is stable; and after many ages, the joys will be as savory and satisfying as if they had been but that moment first tasted by our hungry appetites. When the glory of the Lord shall rise upon you, it shall be so far from ever setting, that after millions of years are expired, as numerous as the sands on the seashore, the sun, in the light of whose countenance you shall live, shall be as bright as at the first appearance; he will be so far from ceasing to flow, that he will flow as strong, as full, as at the first communication of himself in glory to the creature. God, therefore, as sitting upon his throne of grace, and acting according to his covenant, is like a jasper-stone, which is of a green color, a color always delightful (Rev. 4:3); because God is always vigorous and flourishing; a pure act of life, sparkling new and fresh rays of life and light to the creature, flourishing with a perpetual spring, and contenting the most capacious desire; forming your interest, pleasure, and satisfaction; with an infinite variety, without any change or succession; he will have variety to increase delights, and eternity to perpetuate them; this will be the fruit of the enjoyment of an infinite and eternal God: he is not a cistern, but a fountain.[5]

ENJOY HIS PRESENCE

Oh, dear friend, do you hear those words by Stephen Charnock? How profound and deep they are in revealing the majesty of the eternal nature of God, your El Olam. You may even want to read through the words again, slowly, drinking in each phrase and thinking about what it means for your own life.

Notice that Abraham planted a tamarisk tree and then called on El Olam. Commemorating who God is with a physical act such as planting a tree was, for Abraham, an act of worship and remembrance of his great God. The tamarisk tree possesses rich, green foliage and provides constant, welcome shade from the heat of the sun. Abraham recognized the constancy and reliability of his God—He is El Olam, the eternal God. Abraham had just made a covenant with an earthly king, but he recognized he had a much greater covenant, an eternal one from his eternal God. What a sense of security his friendship with God must have provided for him. Just imagine having a friendship with your God—a friendship that lasts forever. Will you take time now to celebrate your eternal friendship with your Lord? Declare it in prayer to Him, remind yourself again and again of this most precious relationship, and then talk to the world about it. Close your quiet time by writing a prayer to your eternal Friend.

REST IN HIS LOVE

"No longer do I call you slaves, for the slave does not know what his master is doing; but I have called you friends, for all things that I have heard from My Father I have made known to you" (John 15:15).

THE TRIUMPH OF A GREAT TRUST

With respect to the promise of God, he did not waver in unbelief but
grew strong in faith, giving glory to God, and being fully assured
that what God had promised, He was able also to perform.

ROMANS 4:20-21

PREPARE YOUR HEART

God revealed Himself through many different names to His friend Abraham. In doing so, God showed Himself to be more than Abraham could imagine, having more facets than the most brilliant of diamonds. James Montgomery Boice says this about God's many names:

> The truth of the matter is that the Bible is one book, given by the one true God through human writers, and that the names of God, far from reflecting diverse gods or sources, are actually names given by God himself to reveal his true nature and attributes. There are many names for God because God is so great he cannot adequately be described by one name or even a dozen names. In fact, even the names we have do not exhaust him. They exhaust us—we will be able to spend an eternity learning of their full implications—but they do not exhaust the Inexhaustible.[6]

Abraham was called to a great task requiring a great trust in God and resulting in a great triumph. Paul tells us that Abraham responded dramatically to his great God because he "did not waver in unbelief but grew strong in faith, giving glory to God, and being fully assured that what God had promised, He was able also to perform" (Romans 4:20-21). Abraham learned to trust in God's names year after year, names such as *El Elyon, El Shaddai,* and *Adonai.* Of all the names of God revealed to Abraham, one stands out because of the nature of the life circumstance surrounding it.

Has God ever asked you to loosen your grip on something or someone you dearly love? He sometimes calls us to a dramatic surrender of a dream or desire, a person or relationship, or a place or possession. Dwight Hervey Small offers this comment:

God tests us to prove and draw out our love for Him. In that process He illumines our competing loves, so that we must evaluate them in relation to our love for Him. His ultimate question is this: Will our love for Him be so transcendant over all competing loves that we may be willingly dispossessed of anything that might hinder our being possessed by Him? The outstanding illustration Scripture gives us of this intimate interconnection of faith and love in the life of victorious obedience is, of course, Abraham.[7]

God asked Abraham to surrender his beloved son Isaac. This was particularly devastating for Abraham because it challenged everything God had promised. Isaac was God's miraculous gift to Abraham and Sarah, the beginning of the fulfillment of one of God's great promises—a multitude of descendants. In Genesis 22 we see Abraham's bewildering test, his phenomenal trust, and his incredible triumph through the revelation of a new name of God—Yahweh Jireh. Let this encourage you when you are in the trial of your faith: Some of the greatest triumphs are possible only through a great test of faith.

As you begin your time with the Lord, do you sense God asking you to loosen your grip on anything in your own life that is competing with your love for Him? Will you draw near to Him now and ask Him to speak to you during your quiet time? You might want to begin by writing a prayer to the Lord on a journal page in the back of this book.

READ AND STUDY GOD'S WORD

1. Oh, what a day it was when God gave Isaac to Sarah and Abraham, who were well past the age of childbearing. God had promised them a son (Genesis 17:19), and He fulfilled that promise through the birth of Isaac (Genesis 21:2). According to Genesis 21:8, Isaac "grew and was weaned, and Abraham made a great feast on the day that Isaac was weaned." Just imagine how much Abraham and Sarah loved their son, Isaac. We are told in Genesis 22:1 that God then tested Abraham. Read Genesis 22:1-2 and write out everything you learn about this test.

2. Place yourself in Abraham's shoes. Imagine what his experience must have been like. Read Genesis 22:3-13 and write out your most significant insights about the character of Abraham in response to God's request.

3. It has been said that the New Testament is in the Old *contained* and that the Old Testament is in the New *explained*. In the hall of fame of faith in Hebrews 11, we learn what was going on in the mind and heart of Abraham. Read Hebrews 11:17-19 and record everything you learn about Abraham.

4. Abraham discovered a new name for God that day, and oh, what a powerful name it is for you. Read Genesis 22:14 and write out the name Abraham gave to the place of the test of his faith.

5. The Hebrew words translated "The Lord Will Provide" are *Yahweh Jireh*. From this name you learn that God is the supplier of all your needs, providing in the midst of every test of your faith. Paul expressed his own trust in Yahweh Jireh when he said, "But I have received everything in full and have an abundance; I am amply supplied...And my God will supply all your needs according to His riches in glory in Christ Jesus" (Philippians 4:18-19). How might your thoughts, feelings, or actions change as you become convinced that God will provide for you regardless of what you face in your own life today?

ADORE GOD IN PRAYER

> O Holy Father, make me humble and unselfish. Give me a childlike faith to receive what you offer and to bear what you ordain; and may a new sense of your presence and power, through the Holy Spirit, stay with me.[8]
>
> F.B. MEYER

YIELD YOURSELF TO GOD

Meditate on these words by Dwight Hervey Small:

> When God tests His children, He knows how they will behave and what the outcome will be. His purpose in testing us is to strengthen us, to sustain us, and to teach us how faithful He is. He plans for us to pass the test so that He can equip us for extraordinary witness to His power, for growth in faith, and that we might develop the enduring quality of love...

For a while, earthly love and heavenly love became rivals. What a devastating test! The only trial in all history which surpassed the agony of Abraham's was Calvary itself…

God began His work on the circumference of Abraham's life and relationships. From there He moved to the very center of his life. In faith and love, Abraham had proved his willingness to be dispossessed of everything for God. Would he willingly be dispossessed of Isaac also?…

Abraham's faith held firm and his love for God did not waver. Divinely enabled in his moment of utter weakness, he replied to his son's shattering question, "God will provide himself the lamb." His answer to Isaac did not lessen his sense of sacrifice, but it did reveal his faith. His obedient faith rested on a divine paradox. Its culmination was trusting God implicitly in spite of seeming contradiction and apparent impossibility…

When God had led His friend at last to the point of no retreat, He acted. Abraham's obedience was completed the very instant his inward surrender was completed. From that moment, God counted it to him as accomplished…Abraham's faith and love were rewarded. He received back the surrendered treasure, made more precious for having been laid upon the altar of sacrifice…

When we ourselves have given our dearest and costliest to God, surrendering all to His will with unreserved love, will He not give back to us in some new way?… However He chooses to do it, God gives us more than we can ever give to Him.[9]

ENJOY HIS PRESENCE

Dear friend, have you experienced or are you experiencing a testing of your own faith? How does Abraham's example help you and urge you on to a higher and greater faith in your Lord? How does knowing Yahweh Jireh, the Lord who provides, encourage you today? In what ways do you need a new and greater trust in Yahweh Jireh? Write your thoughts in the space provided.

REST IN HIS LOVE

"Abraham called the name of that place The LORD Will Provide, as it is said to this day, 'In the mount of the LORD it will be provided'" (Genesis 22:14).

DEVOTIONAL READING
BY A.W. TOZER

When the Bible has led us to God and we have experienced God in the crisis of encounter, then the Bible has done its first work. That it will continue to do God's work in Christian lives should be evident...

What higher privilege and experience is granted to mankind on earth than to be admitted into the circle of the friends of God? Abraham, called in the Bible the father of the faithful, demonstrated in many ways that he had experienced the reality of another and better world. He saw that sphere in which a living God reigns and rules and still encourages men and women to become His friends. God, being perfect, has capacity for perfect friendships...

It is well for us to remember that Divine-human friendship originated with God. Had God not first said, *You are My friends,* it would be inexcusably brash for any man to say, *I am a friend of God.* But since God claims us for His friends, it is an act of unbelief to deny the offer of such a relationship. When we consider the reality of this God-mankind relationship, we are considering the truth and reality of genuine Christian experience. Genuine Christian experience must always include an encounter with God Himself. The spiritual giants of old were those who at some time became acutely conscious of the presence of God. They maintained that consciousness for the rest of their lives.[10]

Will you, dear friend, come boldly to God as your Friend? Take some time now to write about all that you have learned this week. What has been most significant to you? Close by writing a prayer to the Lord.

BEHOLD HIS BEAUTY WITH THE PEOPLE WHO LIVED WITH GOD

The fire of God's Presence needs no fuel. Yield yourself to Him; and if you should ever be tempted to fear that you cannot retain His mighty indwelling by your vows, prayers, or tears, remember that this fire needs no fuel, that it is not by our works of righteousness, but by His grace that He comes to dwell with us and in us. You need supply nothing, but a humble, lowly, penitent, and obedient heart.

F.B. MEYER

THE DIVINE INTERRUPTION OF GOD

The angel of the LORD appeared to him in a blazing fire from the midst of a bush; and he looked, and behold, the bush was burning with fire, yet the bush was not consumed.

EXODUS 3:2

PREPARE YOUR HEART

What a gift the Bible is! In it you are accorded the great privilege of a glimpse into the very heart of God Himself. And when a man or a woman gazes upon the beauty of God, the result is humble worship. Isaiah fell on his face at the revelation of God. John fell at the feet of Jesus when he saw Him in all His glory.

A.W. Tozer spent many a morning on the beach at Lake Michigan contemplating the majesty of God. The deeper Tozer dared to go in plumbing the truths from God's Word about Himself, the more Tozer worshipped. And often, there along the shores of the vast lake on the coast of Chicago, Tozer was on his face before his Holy God. In his first editorial for *Alliance Weekly* magazine, dated June 3, 1950, he wrote, "It will cost something to walk slow in the parade of the ages, while excited men of time rush about confusing motion with progress. But it will pay in the long run and the true Christian is not much interested in anything short of that." Tozer was a man of God, and in fact, his tombstone bears the inscription, "A.W. Tozer—A Man of God."

The truth is that God longs to dwell with His people. The fulfillment of God's desire is described in the words heard from God's throne, "Behold, the tabernacle of God is among men, and He will dwell among them, and they shall be His people, and God Himself will be among them" (Revelation 21:3). The unabashed love of God is written all across the pages of Scripture.

God's love is so great and His desire for His people is so deep that He will interrupt their lives. Why? So His people can know Him. So they can experience all they were created to enjoy. And so they might enjoy the benefits of their relationship with God, including eternal life. You might think of God's interruption as His divine initiative reaching out to give you more than you could have ever hoped for in your life.

Probably one of the most spectacular interruptions by God occurred one day when He appeared in a flame in a bush on the top of a mountain in the wilderness. Moses was just going about his father-in-law's business, tending a flock of sheep. In the midst of his daily routine, he saw a bush that began to burn but did not burn up—it kept burning and burning. How did Moses respond? And what happened as a result? That is the subject of your quiet times this week. Ask God to speak to you in His Word and open your eyes so that you might see amazing and wonderful things, truths that He longs for you to see (Psalm 119:18).

READ AND STUDY GOD'S WORD

1. You have a great claim to fame when you are called a man or woman of God. Moses is called the man of God more than once in Scripture (Deuteronomy 33:1; Joshua 14:6; 1 Chronicles 23:14; 2 Chronicles 30:16; Ezra 3:2; Psalm 90:1). What makes someone a man or woman of God? A primary quality of such a man or woman is the habit of spiritual receptivity and response. When God initiates a relationship, the man or woman of God responds and draws near. The blessed promise in James 4:8 invites us, "Draw near to God and He will draw near to you." Read Exodus 3:1-6 and record all that you see about God and how He initiated a relationship with Moses.

2. Read Exodus 3:1-6 again and record all that you see about Moses' response to the divine interruption and the initiative of God.

3. Summarize in two or three sentences your most significant insights about Moses' encounter with God.

ADORE GOD IN PRAYER

Have you learned this great quality of spiritual receptivity and response? Will you draw near to God now as Moses did when he said, "I must turn aside now and see this marvelous sight" (Exodus 3:3)? And then will you talk with the Lord and pray the prayer of Moses, "Here I am" (verse 4)? Talk with your Lord, realizing that He loves you, wants to be close to you, and longs for you to know Him and walk with Him.

YIELD YOURSELF TO GOD

Meditate on these insights by A.W. Tozer:

> Previously, God had been just a good and pleasant idea to Moses. The idea of God is a distant and nebulous concept, and the average person tries to deal with it on the basis of intellect. As an orthodox Hebrew, Moses' idea of receiving God had been only in the intellectual sense. Now he finds himself in the very presence of the living God. The fire in the bush was God dwelling within the fire and shining out through the fire. Now he experiences God personally. God becomes vital and living. This incident brings to our minds the fact that there are two kinds of knowledge. There is a knowledge that comes from description. One person describes a thing to another, and the other person gains some knowledge of it. We can give knowledge to others by description. Then there is the knowledge that comes from experience. It is possible to describe a battle fought in a war. But the soldier who has gone through the hell of actual shot and shell and fire knows the battle by personal experience. The memory is for a lifetime. It is something he cannot escape. It was in this sense that Moses met God at the burning bush. He was a man experiencing the presence of God. To Moses, God was no longer an idea from history but a living Person willing to become involved with His creation, mankind.[1]

ENJOY HIS PRESENCE

In what ways has God interrupted your life and expressed His divine initiative and prerogative to display His majesty and glory to you that you might draw near and know Him? How have you experienced God as who He is, more than an idea, but the triune, living God? How can you respond to Him today and say "Yes, Lord, here I am"? Write your thoughts in the space provided.

REST IN HIS LOVE

"Draw near to God and He will draw near to you" (James 4:8).

TRUSTING IN THE GOD WHO SEES

The LORD said, "I have surely seen the affliction of My people who are in Egypt, and have given heed to their cry because of their taskmasters, for I am aware of their sufferings."

EXODUS 3:7

PREPARE YOUR HEART

George Beverly Shea, vocalist for the Billy Graham Evangelistic Association, was visiting a friend in Florida. The friend's brother-in-law pulled up to the house in a large red 18-wheel truck. Noticing Shea's interest in the truck, the driver called out, "Jump in." Riding in an 18-wheeler was a first for Shea, so he excitedly climbed into the truck.

While they drove around, the truck driver quietly began opening up his heart. He said, "You know, driving this rig mile after mile, it gets quite tiring and lonely, especially after the sun goes down...I hear you in the dark of night as I travel down the highways, often listening to the *Hour of Decision.* I can hardly see the road after you sing songs like 'Lord, I'm Coming Home.'"[2]

After the heartfelt exchange, Shea and the truck driver prayed together. The driver's life was changed forever as he gave his heart to the Lord. Only God knew how much meeting George Beverly Shea would mean to that truck driver. And how did God know? Because He sees everything, and He cares about everyone.

Oh, what a happy day it is when a man or woman of God realizes that God sees, God knows, and God cares! God's people, the people of Israel, were about to discover that He knew every agony of their suffering and had heard their cries. To remind His people of His discernment and comprehension of their circumstances, and His immense care and comfort on their behalf, He revealed one of His names: *El Roi* (the God who sees). God's sight extends far beyond mere recognition; He acts on behalf of those He sees. Such was the case for the people of Israel. And even more amazing to comprehend, such is the case for you.

READ AND STUDY GOD'S WORD

1. Once Moses turned aside to look, God called out his name, "Moses, Moses!" When Moses realized God was speaking to him, he "hid his face, for he was afraid to look at God" (Exodus 3:6). Then God began sharing His heart with Moses, preparing the way for His certain and direct

call of Moses to a great task. Read Exodus 3:7-10 and record all that you learn about God from His words to Moses.

Who God is:

What God does:

What God says:

2. God makes a powerful statement about the sufferings of His people. He says, "I have surely seen the affliction of My people who are in Egypt, and have given heed to their cry because of their taskmasters, for I am aware of their sufferings. So I have come down to deliver them from the power of the Egyptians, and to bring them up from that land to a good and spacious land, to a land flowing with milk and honey" (Exodus 3:7-8). As you think about these words, describe what happens when God sees the affliction of His people.

3. God's sight is not simply a bare recognition. When God sees, He acts. And in the case of the people of Israel, He delivered. The Israelites were not the first to understand this quality about God. An obscure woman, an Egyptian maid named Hagar, was given the great privilege of hearing from God and learning the name *El Roi* (Genesis 16:13). Read Genesis 16:1-15 and record what you learn about who God is, what God does, and what God says. (Note that the angel of the Lord is the Lord Himself—see Genesis 16:13.)

Who God is:

What God does:

What God says:

4. In what way do you need to run to El Roi today? In what unseen and obscure corners of your life do you need His help and deliverance?

ADORE GOD IN PRAYER

Pray the words of Spurgeon today:

> Blessed be Thy Name, Thou ever-living God…We look up to Thee with joyful confidence, knowing that Thou art an inexhaustible fountain of every good thing, and believing that Thou wilt supply our need out of the riches of Thy fullness of glory by Christ Jesus. Wilt Thou refresh our souls? We come as the Children of Israel came to the wells of Elim, and we would now sit by the palm-trees thereof. Let our souls gather strength. Give comfort to the mourners; give rebuke to those that slumber, and a word in season to everyone…May there be food fitted for strong men, as well as milk for babes, and may we all of us retire from the Master's house feeling that He has satisfied us with good things, and made us rejoice in Himself. Our Father, hear and bless us for Jesus' sake. Amen.[3]

YIELD YOURSELF TO GOD

> Our Lord's sight is insight. The majority of us see, but only a few perceive…The Master not only feels, He works; He not only sympathizes, He serves.[4]

> JOHN HENRY JOWETT

> He knows. He sees. There is no look heavenward, there is no desire heavenward, there is no aspiration after goodness, there is not an honest struggle for a nobler life in your heart, in your home, anywhere, everywhere, but what God sees and God knows.[5]

> GYPSY SMITH

ENJOY HIS PRESENCE

Knowing and trusting El Roi will change your life forever. When you draw near to El Roi and call out to Him, you will discover His help in a time of trouble. He is a "God of deliverances" (Psalm 68:20). How do you need El Roi today? Turn to the prayer pages in the back of this book and devote a page to all your needs in prayer to El Roi. Then watch to see what He will do in response to your prayers. Always remember the words He said to Moses: "I have surely seen the affliction of My people...and have given heed to their cry...for I am aware of their sufferings. So I have come down to deliver them" (Exodus 3:7-8). Depend on the assuring words of your God today, especially the word *surely*. He surely sees you, and you can count on Him.

REST IN HIS LOVE

"Then she called the name of the Lord who spoke to her, 'You are a God who sees'" (Genesis 16:13).

TRUSTING IN THE GREAT I AM

"Now they may say to me, 'What is His name?' What shall I say to them?" God said to Moses, "I AM WHO I AM"; and He said, "Thus you shall say to the sons of Israel, 'I AM has sent me to you.'"

EXODUS 3:13-14

PREPARE YOUR HEART

People cannot trust what they do not know. God called Moses to a monumental task requiring enormous trust. Moses' first question of God was related to His character. Moses wanted to know who God was and asked a bold and courageous question of God. He asked God what he should say if the people asked, "What is His name?" What a good question. And oh, what an answer God gave to Moses that day. Today, as you prepare for time alone with the Lord, turn the eyes of your heart to God and ask Him that same question: *What is Your name?*

READ AND STUDY GOD'S WORD

1. When Moses dared to ask God His name, he received more than he could have expected. God chose at that very moment to tell Moses His eternal name *Yahweh*. He then explained how important this name was. He said, "This is My name forever, and this is My memorial-name to all generations" (Exodus 3:15). Read Exodus 3:11-13 and describe how Moses must have felt after hearing God's plan and His call.

2. God responded to Moses' question in great detail. Read Exodus 3:14-17 and write everything you learn about God.

Who God is:

What God does:

What God says:

3. In the *Trusting in the Names of God* 30-day journey, you learn this about *Yahweh:*

When God revealed His name, *I AM WHO I AM,* He spoke His name using Hebrew verbs, not nouns. The verb forms are imperfect tense, implying continuing, unfinished action: "I am the one who always is." *Yahweh* is often called the *Tetragrammaton* or "four-lettered name"; the Hebrew word translated "I AM" is *YHVH,* transliterated *Yahweh. Yahweh* is so sacred a word in rabbinical writings that it is distinguished with euphemistic expressions such as "the name," "the unutterable name," and "the holy name." Jewish reverence for Yahweh is so great that authors and writers frequently refrained from putting the name into print or speaking the name aloud.[6] Perhaps most telling, *Yahweh* is used 6823 times in the Old Testament alone and is rendered *LORD,* usually in small capital letters, befitting its sacred and personal nature.

(Note: The original pronunciation for YHVH, known to the Patriarchs and to Moses, has been lost following the destruction of Jerusalem in AD 70. Some scholars refer to this name of God as *Yahweh* and others as *Jehovah.* Since the construct form *Yah* is most likely part of the original pronunciation, we will refer to YHVH as *Yahweh.*)

Don't you find it interesting that God's name *Yahweh* is a verb, not a noun? He is implying that He is everything you need for every circumstance of your life. He will meet your deepest needs. Look at the following verses and write out everything you learn about *Yahweh (LORD).*

Psalm 34:19

Psalm 37:18

Psalm 145:14-18

Isaiah 40:28-31

Isaiah 43:1

Jeremiah 29:11-13

4. Summarize what you have learned about Yahweh from your time in God's Word today.

ADORE GOD IN PRAYER

Use the words of Amy Carmichael as your prayer today, expressing your desire to know your God:

> God of the heights, austere, inspiring,
> Thy word hath come to me;
> O let no selfish aims, conspiring,
> Distract my soul from Thee.
> Loosen me from Things of Time—
> Strengthen me for steadfast climb.
>
> The temporal would bind my spirit;
> Father, be Thou my stay.
> Show me what flesh cannot inherit,
> Stored for another day.
> Be transparent, Things of Time—
> Looking through you, I would climb.

Now by Thy grace my spirit chooseth
Treasure that shall abide.
The great Unseen, I know, endureth;
My footsteps shall not slide.
Nor for me the Things of Time—
God of mountains, I will climb.[7]

AMY CARMICHAEL

YIELD YOURSELF TO GOD

Meditate on these words by Hannah Whitall Smith:

This, then, is what I mean by God being enough. It is that we find in Him, in the fact of His existence, and of His character, all that we can possibly want for everything. *God is,* must be our answer to every question and every cry of need. If there is any lack in the One who has undertaken to save us, nothing supplementary we can do will avail to make it up; and if there is no lack in Him, then He, of Himself and in Himself, is enough…Therefore, God is enough! God is enough for time, God is enough for eternity. God is *enough!*[8]

ENJOY HIS PRESENCE

What encouragement do you gain from knowing the memorial name of God, *Yahweh?* How do you need Yahweh today? Will you close by writing a prayer to Yahweh, expressing all that is on your heart?

REST IN HIS LOVE

"The LORD is righteous in all His ways and kind in all His deeds. The LORD is near to all who call upon Him, to all who call upon Him in truth" (Psalm 145:17-18).

DARING TO DRAW NEAR

Now therefore, I pray You, if I have found favor in Your sight,
let me know Your ways that I may know You, so that I may find
favor in your sight...I pray You, show me Your glory!

EXODUS 33:13,18

PREPARE YOUR HEART

Life is all about the great adventure of knowing God. God's greatest desire is you. He wants you to know Him and experience an intimate relationship with Him. His invitation to intimacy is written all across the pages of His Word. He says, "Be still, and know that I am God" (Psalm 46:10 NIV). In Jeremiah 9:23-24, God says, "Let not a wise man boast of his wisdom, and let not the mighty man boast of his might, let not a rich man boast of his riches; but let him who boasts boast of this, that he understands and knows Me, that I am the LORD who exercises lovingkindness, justice and righteousness on earth; for I delight in these things." In James 4:8, God promises that when you draw near to Him, He will draw near to you.

Moses, the most humble man on the face of the earth according to Numbers 12:3, understood the heart of God and His desire for an intimate relationship. As humble as he was, he might not have dared to venture out into the vast waters of knowing God had he not already experienced time alone with Him. Moses experienced the rare communion with God afforded to those who will dare to draw near. In Exodus 33:11 we learn that "the LORD used to speak to Moses face to face, just as a man speaks to his friend," and Deuteronomy 34:10 tells us that "no prophet has risen in Israel like Moses, whom the LORD knew face to face." Oh, what powerful words these are to encourage longing hearts to engage in conversation and intimate communion with God. And when you dare to draw near, don't be surprised if God shows you something new about Himself—a new name or a new attribute—something profound that will expand and deepen your relationship with Him.

As you begin your quiet time today, turn to Psalm 90 and meditate on the words written by Moses, the man of God.

READ AND STUDY GOD'S WORD

1. Sometimes God allows you a glimpse into His intimate conversations with rare hearts who knew Him well. Take some time now to read Exodus 33:11-23 and write out what is most significant to you about the conversation between God and Moses.

2. Read Exodus 33:13-19 and write out, word for word, the prayer requests of Moses. Also, note God's response to his requests.

3. God responded to the request of Moses by proclaiming what one commentator calls "the proclamation and implications of His name."[9] Perhaps what God proclaimed might be understood as one of the longest names for God in the Bible. Read Exodus 34:1-7 and write out everything you learn about God (see especially verses 6-7).

4. How did Moses respond according to Exodus 34:8-9?

5. No man can see the actual face of God and live (Exodus 33:20). When Moses spoke face-to-face with God, that phrase implied intimacy—a heart-to-heart relationship. And yet Moses boldly prayed, "Show me your glory." The Hebrew word translated "glory" is *kabod* and refers to the splendor and majesty of God's presence. Sometimes God will turn down the volume on His glory so you can catch just a glimpse of His magnificent beauty. Look at the following verses and record what you learn about your own experience of the glory of God.

1 Corinthians 3:16

2 Corinthians 3:18

2 Corinthians 4:6-7

ADORE GOD IN PRAYER

Will you take some time to be still in the solitude of this moment and pray the words of Moses today? "Now therefore, I pray You, if I have found favor in Your sight, let me know Your ways that I may know You, so that I may find favor in Your sight…I pray You, show me Your glory" (Exodus 33:13,18).

YIELD YOURSELF TO GOD

Think about these words by F.B. Meyer:

Perhaps Moses, as he entered the cloud, expected that the Almighty would pass before him, riding upon a cherub, flying upon the wings of the wind, girt with rainbow and storm, while the thunder rolled as drums in his march. But lo! he seemed to stand in a ravine, upon a ledge of rock, shadowed by a hand, whilst through that mountain-rent passed the Divine procession; and a voice, still, sweet, penetrating, told that God was Love. Mark the progress of revelation to the adoring soul. In Horeb, Moses had stood in the outer court, to learn that God is changeless. In the giving of the Law he had stood in the effulgent glory of the Holy Place, to learn that God is righteous. Now he was admitted to the inner shrine, to learn that the Lord God was merciful and gracious, long-suffering, and abundant in goodness and truth. The answers to our prayers for spiritual vision may not always come as we expect. But, however they come, come they will. None of those who wait for Him shall be ashamed. He will satisfy desires which He has Himself implanted…

The face of Moses shone: and did not his heart and life shine also? Could it have been otherwise? Linen in which the housewife has laid rosemary and lavender will smell fragrantly; ordinary iron placed near a magnet becomes magnetic; those that are in king's courts catch a refined and courteous mien; the friend of wise men gets wisdom; the members of a closely-knit family contract by association some tiny gesture, a peculiarity which betrays their oneness; it is proverbial how on the faces of an aged couple there is seen a strong resemblance, so that each reflects the other. And it is impossible for us to be much with God without becoming godly, i.e., God-like...

That blessed vision which of old was given only to the great leader of Israel, is now within reach of each individual believer. The Gospel has no fences to keep off the crowds from the mount of vision; the lowliest and most unworthy of its children may pass upward where the shining glory is to be seen. We are not living in the morning, when the rays of the sun reach only the elect spirits that tower above the rest; but in the noon, when every tiny flower and hidden nook lies in full view of the meridian sun. *We all, are changed.*[10]

ENJOY HIS PRESENCE

What a powerful revelation God displayed to Moses that day on Mt. Sinai. God's proclamation to Moses was so important and profound that it was frequently recalled in other places throughout the Old Testament (see Numbers 14:18; Nehemiah 9:17; Psalm 86:15; 103:8; 145:8; Joel 2:13; Jonah 4:2). The repetition of this proclamation and other names of God throughout the Old Testament demonstrates the importance of discovering God's names, drawing near to His names that we might understand God better, declaring His names as many others did throughout the Old Testament, depending on His names in trust of who He is, and finally delighting in His names in praise and worship.

As you close your quiet time with the Lord today, what is the most important truth about God you have learned from the life of Moses?

REST IN HIS LOVE

"But we all, with unveiled face, beholding as in a mirror the glory of the Lord, are being transformed into the same image from glory to glory, just as from the Lord, the Spirit" (2 Corinthians 3:18).

TRUSTING IN THE LIVING GOD

Joshua said, "By this you shall know that the living God is among you."

JOSHUA 3:10

PREPARE YOUR HEART

What happens when a person sees God at work in the life of another? That person becomes bold and courageous for the Lord and sees that God is real and personal rather than distant and unconcerned. The perfect example is Joshua, the servant of Moses. We see in Exodus 33:11 that "the LORD used to speak to Moses face to face, just as a man speaks to his friend." But then we see something so very interesting and incredibly important. Another person was looking on, drinking in, and learning—Joshua. "When Moses returned to the camp, his servant Joshua, the son of Nun, a young man, would not depart from the tent" (Exodus 33:11). What profound training for one who would be the next leader of God's people! Ask God to speak to your heart today and show you the importance and value of having friends and leaders who demonstrate their trust in the living God.

READ AND STUDY GOD'S WORD

1. Following the death of Moses, the Lord called Joshua to be the next leader of His people. Read Joshua 1:1-9 and write out your most significant insight from these verses.

2. Joshua challenged the people of Israel to launch out on the promises of God. He referred to the presence of God among them when he said, "By this you shall know that the living God is among you" (Joshua 3:10). The Hebrew words translated "the living God" are *El Hay* and characterize "the Lord as one who lives and acts, contrasted with the pagan gods, who are 'dead,' that is, unable to act and save their peoples."[11] Others throughout the Bible knew El Hay, the living God. Look at the following verses and record what you learn about El Hay and your response to Him.

Psalm 84:2

Jeremiah 10:10

Daniel 6:26

3. The gods of this world are in fact no gods at all, but idols. We must guard against idolatry in any form by worshipping only the one true God. Look at the following verses and record what you learn about idolatry:

Exodus 20:4

Psalm 115:1-11

2 Corinthians 6:16-18

4. Think about your own culture and world. What gods or idols do people worship today? What must believers guard against in the world?

ADORE GOD IN PRAYER

Pray these words from "The Pledge of Trust" by Bryan Jeffery Leech in your time of prayer:

Father, during this coming week there may be times when I shall not be able to sense Your presence or to be aware of Your nearness.

- When I am lonely and by myself, I trust You to be my companion.

- When I am tempted to sin, I trust You to keep me from it.

- When I am depressed and anxious, I trust You to lift my spirits.

- When I am crushed by responsibility and overwhelmed by the demands of people on my time, I trust You to give me poise and a sense of purpose.

- When I am rushed and running, I trust You to make me still inside.

- When I forget You, I trust that You will never forget me.

- When I forget others, I trust You to prompt me to think of them.

- When You take something or someone from me that I want to keep; when You remove the props I lean on for comfort in place of You; when You refuse to respond to my questions and to answer my too-selfish prayers, I will trust You even then.

AMEN.[12]

YIELD YOURSELF TO GOD

Draw near and learn more as George Mueller shares the following about El Hay, the living God:

> We know it is written "the living God"; but in our daily life there is scarcely anything we practically so much lose sight of as the fact that God is *the living God;* that He is now whatever He was three or four thousand years since; that He has the same sovereign power, the same love towards those who love and serve Him as He ever had and that He will do for them now what He did for others two, three, four thousand years ago, simply because He is the living God, the unchanging One. Oh, how therefore we should confide in Him, and in our darkest moments never lose sight of the fact that He is still and ever will be the living God! Be assured, if you walk with Him and look to Him and expect help from Him, He will never fail you. An older brother who has known the Lord for forty-four years, who writes this, says to you for your encouragement that He has never failed him. In the greatest difficulties, in the heaviest trials, in the deepest poverty and necessities, He has never failed me; but because I was enabled by His grace to trust Him He has always appeared for my help. I delight in speaking well of His name.[13]

ENJOY HIS PRESENCE

What is your most significant insight from the life of Joshua and his relationship with El Hay, the living God? Write a prayer of trust in the living God as you close your quiet time with Him today.

REST IN HIS LOVE

"My soul longed and even yearned for the courts of the LORD; my heart and my flesh sing for joy to the living God" (Psalm 84:2).

DEVOTIONAL READING
BY F.B. MEYER

If we garner every opportunity, cultivate every faculty, and keep our faces ever toward the mountain of communion, we shall infallibly find that the heart which yearns for the vision shall not be left without the vision for which it yearns; and that the yearning is the unconscious awakening of the soul to the fact that it is standing on the threshold of the highest privilege possible to man. It is thus that a babe awakens to a mother's tenderness, and a maiden becomes conscious of the great destiny to which an unexpected love, which has stolen so mysteriously upon her, beckons. Oh, these mysterious risings of the water in the river where the barges lie, bearing them up on their arms, rattling their chains, straining their cords, and bringing them an assurance of the swell and fulness and glory of the great ocean, which calls to them to launch forth on its broad expanse and fathomless depths! And the Lord said unto Moses, "I will do this thing also that thou hast spoken; for thou hast found grace in My sight. Be ready in the morning, and come up in the morning unto Mount Sinai"…

We must dare to be alone…Valuable as are the prolific opportunities for Christian culture and service which surround us, they will be disastrous indeed in their effect if they rob us of the time that we should otherwise spend with God, or give us a distaste for lonely heart-fellowship. Let the first moments of the day, when the heart is fresh, be given to God. Never see the face of man till you have seen the King. Dare to be much alone on the Mount.[14]

Take some time now to write about all that you have learned this week. What has been most significant to you? Write a prayer to the Lord, expressing all that is on your heart.

BEHOLD HIS BEAUTY WITH THE PROPHETS, WHO SPOKE FOR GOD

What makes life worthwhile is having a big enough objective, something which catches our imagination and lays hold of our allegiance; and this the Christian has, in a way that no other man has. For what higher, more exalted, and more compelling goal can there be than to know God?

J.I. Packer

TRUSTING IN YOUR REDEEMER

I will help you, declares the LORD, and your
Redeemer is the Holy One of Israel.
ISAIAH 41:14

PREPARE YOUR HEART

Probably few shared the heart of God more intimately than the prophets, those men who spoke for God to the people of God. This week we will enjoy a rare glimpse into the hearts of Isaiah, Jeremiah, Ezekiel, Daniel, and Zechariah, and we will think more deeply about some of the names of God these men knew and trusted. To be called by God as His prophet was a privilege. Walter Kaiser, in his book *Back Toward the Future*, helps us understand the role of the prophet in God's plan:

> God disclosed his secrets to his sons and daughters through his apostles and prophets…Prophecy is not a sterile, remote subject which has an interesting trivia list. It is a call to action based on the certainty of the future acts of God in space and time. It is a call to repentance based on the present drift of an evil society and a backsliding church. It is a call to faith and belief in the living God who is doing all things well after the counsel of his own wise and holy will.[1]

Peter encourages us to pay attention to what the prophets have said:

> So we have the prophetic word made more sure, to which you do well to pay attention as to a lamp shining in a dark place, until the day dawns and the morning star arises in your hearts. But know this first of all, that no prophecy of Scripture is a matter of one's own interpretation, for no prophecy was ever made by an act of human will, but men moved by the Holy Spirit spoke from God (2 Peter 1:19-21).

The Word of God is a light shining in this world, showing us who God is, what He does, and what He says.

Oh, how the prophets knew and trusted their God! And so must you, especially for such a time as this. Draw near to the Lord now and ask God to speak to your heart as you discover His names, draw near to His names, declare His names, depend on His names, and delight in His names.

READ AND STUDY GOD'S WORD

1. The prophet Isaiah is the subject of your time in God's Word today. He lived during the reigns of Uzziah, Jotham, Ahaz, and Hezekiah, all kings of Judah (Isaiah 1:1). Look at God's call of Isaiah in Isaiah 6:1-8 and write what you see and learn about God.

2. God revealed Himself to Isaiah through the name *Redeemer*. In fact, you are going to take a bit more time than usual in the Word because this name of God is so incredibly important to think about and understand. God gives us His name through Isaiah when He says, " 'I will help you,' declares the LORD, 'and your Redeemer is the Holy One of Israel' " (Isaiah 41:14). The Hebrew word translated "Redeemer" is *ga'al* and means to redeem, ransom, and exercise the responsibility of a kinsman.[2] The redeemer pays the purchase price to redeem back lost property, lost freedom, and lost rights. The ultimate result of our Redeemer's payment is our deliverance.

Look at the following verses and record what you learn about the Lord as your Redeemer:

Job 19:25

Isaiah 54:5

3. In the Bible, a kinsman-redeemer is one who redeems his relative from difficulty or danger. The Bible's most beautiful picture of a kinsman-redeemer is seen in the book of Ruth. Following the tragic deaths of the husbands of Naomi and her daughter-in-law Ruth, Boaz, the kinsman-redeemer, steps in and acquires the land belonging to Naomi and takes Ruth as his wife. Read Ruth 4:13-15 and write out what is most significant to you in this description of Boaz's actions.

4. The Lord is your Redeemer. What does redemption mean for you? The redemption He has accomplished on your behalf is great and powerful and gives you more than you can imagine.

He paid a great purchase price—the death of His Son—and bought your freedom from the slave market of sin and death. Now you may receive forgiveness of sins and eternal life. See these tremendous truths for yourself in God's Word. Look at the following verses and record what you learn about your need for redemption and the price that your Redeemer paid on your behalf.

John 3:16

Romans 3:23-24

Romans 5:6-10

Ephesians 1:7

Colossians 2:13-14

Hebrews 9:12

5. Redemption has been accomplished by Jesus Christ on your behalf. He is your Redeemer. Salvation, forgiveness of sins, and eternal life are yours when you receive His free gift. If you have never established a relationship with God through Jesus Christ and received His gift of forgiveness of sins and eternal life, you can take that step now, using this prayer: *Lord Jesus, I need You. Thank You for dying on the cross for my sins. I invite You now to come into my life, forgive my sins, and make me the person You want me to be. Thank You, Lord. I pray in Jesus' name. Amen.* According to John 1:12, "As many as received Him, to them He gave the right to become children of God, even to those who believe in His name." That can include you!

ADORE GOD IN PRAYER

Use these words by Isaac Watts to thank the Lord, your Redeemer, for all He has done on your behalf:

> When I survey the wondrous cross
> On which the Prince of glory died,
> My richest gain I count but loss,
> And pour contempt on all my pride.
>
> See from His head, His hands, His feet,
> Sorrow and love flow mingled down!
> Did e'er such love and sorrow meet,
> Or thorns compose so rich a crown?
>
> Were the whole realm of nature mine,
> That were a present far too small;
> Love so amazing, so divine,
> Demands my soul, my life, my all.

YIELD YOURSELF TO GOD

Meditate on these words by Martyn Lloyd-Jones about the redemption you have in Christ:

It is what God did at Calvary that produces our forgiveness. Calvary is not merely a proclamation or an announcement of God's love and readiness to forgive; it is God, through what He did in and by His Son on Calvary's Cross, making a way whereby He can reconcile us unto Himself...

The redemption is in Christ Himself. He is not the mere announcement of it; He is it, He Himself is it...He! The Lord Jesus Christ Himself! This can never be repeated too frequently, it can never be emphasized too much. I can put it in the form of a question: Do you believe, do you know that your sins are forgiven? Do you know that God has forgiven you? If you do, I ask this further question—How does God forgive you? Let me ask another question which is still more searching: Do you believe, do you see, and do you know, that it is because of what happened in Christ, and because of that alone, that God has forgiven you? When you think of yourself and of the forgiveness of your sins, do you think solely in terms of the fact that God is love, that God is piteous, and that God is merciful and compassionate? Is Christ merely the greatest statement of God's love and compassion that has ever been made, or did He merely make the greatest statement with respect to it? Or do you see, and know, and rely solely, upon the fact that what happened in Christ is God's way of forgiving? That is the question. "In whom we have redemption through his blood." He is not only a preacher or teacher; He is the salvation.[3]

ENJOY HIS PRESENCE

Dear friend, don't ever forget what your Lord has done for you in accomplishing redemption. And know this, according to 1 Corinthians 6:20: "You have been bought with a price: therefore glorify God in your body." You belong to your Lord. And oh, what a joy to know that you are His. As you think about all these truths, what is your most significant insight today? What does it mean to know the Lord as your Redeemer? How do you need to trust Him today?

REST IN HIS LOVE

"You, O LORD, are our Father, our Redeemer from of old is Your name" (Isaiah 63:16).

TRUSTING IN YAHWEH TSIDKENU, THE LORD YOUR RIGHTEOUSNESS

And this is His name by which He will be called, The LORD our righteousness.

JEREMIAH 23:6

PREPARE YOUR HEART

Often in God's economy the greatest brokenness results in the most profound blessing. Such was the case in the life of Jeremiah, known by many as the weeping prophet. Jeremiah was the Lord's prophet just before the Babylonian captivity and during Babylon's three sieges of Judah. In fact, Jeremiah himself suffered much and was often God's object lesson to the people of Israel, helping them to comprehend the extreme nature of their offense against their holy, just, and righteous God.

Jeremiah wept and grieved deeply as he shared God's heart of brokenness over the sins of His people, but Jeremiah also received a tremendous glimpse into the character of his God. Jeremiah is the one who learned that the greatest boast a person could have was to know God (Jeremiah 9:23-24). And he is the one who discovered that the greatest trust a person could have was trust in God (Jeremiah 17:5-8).

As you begin your quiet time, prepare your heart by meditating on the words of Psalm 4:1-5.

READ AND STUDY GOD'S WORD

1. Begin your study of God's Word today by looking at God's call of Jeremiah in Jeremiah 1:4-10. Write out everything you learn about God.

2. Jeremiah 23:5-6 includes one of God's names: *Yahweh Tsidkenu.* God says, "Behold, the days are coming...when I will raise up for David a righteous Branch; and He will reign as king and act wisely and do justice and righteousness in the land. In His days Judah will be saved, and Israel will dwell securely; and this is His name by which He will be called, 'The LORD our

righteousness.'" Jeremiah gave this prophecy when the kingdom of Judah was near its fall, captivity, and ultimate exile to Babylon. The beauty of this promise is that even in the midst of the coming devastation of Judah, there was still hope, and God's purpose and promise could never be defeated. There was one who would sit on the throne as King, the Lord our righteousness.

We see the fulfillment of this prophecy in Jesus, who "became to us wisdom from God, and righteousness and sanctification, and redemption" (1 Corinthians 1:30). The Hebrew words *Yahweh Tsidkenu* are translated "the Lord our righteousness" and come from the compound of *tsedeq* ("justice, rightness, and conformity to the nature and will of God") and the possessive pronoun *nu* ("our").

The beautiful truth of this name of God is that in ourselves, we could never be righteous or enjoy a right standing before a holy and just God. He gives us what we need and does for us what we can never do for ourselves. Knowing that He is Yahweh Tsidkenu can encourage you today. In fact, you might think of this name as evidence of God's provision of GRACE (God's Riches At Christ's Expense). Look at the following verses and record what you learn about the righteousness you have in Christ:

Romans 3:21-26

2 Corinthians 5:21

3. After reading the verses in Romans 3:21-26 and 2 Corinthians 5:21, how can we, who are sinners, be made righteous?

Adore God in Prayer

Pray the words of Psalm 31:1-3 today:

> In You, O Lord, I have taken refuge;
> Let me never be ashamed;
> In Your righteousness deliver me.
> Incline Your ear to me, rescue me quickly;

Be to me a rock of strength,
A stronghold to save me.
For You are my rock and my fortress;
For Your name's sake You will lead me and guide me.

And then, worship and praise Yahweh Tsidkenu with the words of Psalm 36:5-9:

Your lovingkindness, O LORD, extends to the heavens,
Your faithfulness reaches to the skies.
Your righteousness is like the mountains of God;
Your judgments are like a great deep.
O LORD, You preserve man and beast.
How precious is Your lovingkindness, O God!
And the children of men take refuge in the shadow of Your wings.
They drink their fill of the abundance of Your house;
And You give them to drink of the river of Your delights.
For with You is the fountain of life;
In Your light we see light.

YIELD YOURSELF TO GOD

Think about these words by William Newell:

God, acting in righteousness, reckons righteous the ungodly man who trusts Him: because He places him in the full value of the infinite work of Christ on the cross, and transfers him into Christ Risen, who becomes his righteousness.[4]

J. Vernon McGee expresses the work of Christ this way:

Jesus Christ took my place down here. He, who knew no sin, came that we might be made the righteousness of God in Him. He has given me His place, clothed in His righteousness. He took my hell down here so that I might have His heaven up yonder. He did that for me. Christian friend, have you been able to get out this wonderful Word to anyone else? Whoever you are, wherever you are, however you are, what are you doing today to get this Word of reconciliation out to a lost world? God is reconciled. He is the same yesterday, today, and forever. He feels toward you just as He did the day Christ died on the Cross for you and for all mankind. This is what the world needs to hear from you. The world is reconciled to Him, but they will have to turn around and by faith come to Him. Let's get this word out, my friend.[5]

ENJOY HIS PRESENCE

Do you see the great exchange that has taken place? Christ traded places with you, took your sin on Himself, and paid the penalty for your sin so that He might give you His righteousness, the righteousness of God, forgiveness of sins, and eternal life. Who would do that? Only Yahweh Tsidkenu, the Lord your righteousness. Close your time today by reflecting on these words written by the young Scottish preacher, Robert Murray McCheyne:

> I once was a stranger to grace and to God,
> I knew not my danger, and felt not my load;
> Though friends spoke in rapture of Christ on the tree,
> Jehovah Tsidkenu was nothing to me.
> I oft read with pleasure, to soothe or engage,
> Isaiah's wild measure and John's simple page;
> But e'en when they pictured the blood-sprinkled tree,
> Jehovah Tsidkenu seemed nothing to me.
> Like tears from the daughters of Zion that roll,
> I wept when the waters went over His soul;
> Yet thought not that my sins had nailed to the tree,
> Jehovah Tsidkenu—'twas nothing to me.
> When free grace awoke me, by light from on high,
> Then legal fears shook me, I trembled to die;
> No refuge, no safety in self could I see—
> Jehovah Tsidkenu my Saviour must be.
> My terrors all vanished before the sweet name;
> My guilty fears banished, with boldness I came
> To drink at the fountain, life-giving and free—
> Jehovah Tsidkenu is all things to me.
> Jehovah Tsidkenu! my treasure and boast,
> Jehovah Tsidkenu! I ne'er can be lost;
> In Thee I shall conquer by flood and by field—
> My cable, my anchor, my breastplate and shield!
> Even treading the valley, the shadow of death,

This "watchword" shall rally my faltering breath;
For while from life's fever my God sets me free,
Jehovah Tsidkenu my death-song shall be.[6]

REST IN HIS LOVE

"He made Him who knew no sin to be sin on our behalf, so that we might become the righteousness of God in Him" (2 Corinthians 5:21).

TRUSTING IN YAHWEH SHAMMAH, THE LORD IS THERE

The name of the city from that day shall be, "The LORD is there."

Ezekiel 48:35

Prepare Your Heart

Amanda Smith, born in 1837, was a freed slave used mightily of the Lord to bring times of refreshing to many church congregations where she spoke. At the age of 19, filled with a great longing for God and His presence in her life, Amanda went down in a cellar to pray. *O Lord,* she prayed, *if You will help me, I will believe You.* Peace and joy flooded her soul, and the burden of sin was gone. By the age of 32, Amanda was a widow, and she began an evangelistic ministry. God used her as a powerful witness for Him in America, England, India, and Africa. God's strength, power, and especially His presence were experienced by many men and women whenever she spoke in churches.

Life transformation happens when God is at work in and through lives. Revival occurs when people repent and return to the Lord. Luke gives the great result of God's work: "Times of refreshing may come from the presence of the Lord" (Acts 3:19).

Oh, how life transforming is the presence of the Lord! Ezekiel was a priest called by God to be a prophet (Ezekiel 1:3). Ezekiel may have had hopes of serving the Lord as a priest in the temple in Jerusalem, but his service to God as a prophet was his calling, and he was taken into exile to Babylon. He never again saw Jerusalem or the temple, for both were destroyed by Nebuchadnezzar in 586 BC. Even though he never again saw the earthly temple, he was given a vision of another temple, a new Jerusalem, and a name of God he would never forget: *Yahweh Shammah,* "the LORD is there."

Read and Study God's Word

1. Ezekiel received remarkable visions from God. His initial vision is described in the first chapter of Ezekiel with these words: "As the appearance of the rainbow in the clouds on a rainy

day, so was the appearance of the surrounding radiance. Such was the appearance of the likeness of the glory of the LORD. And when I saw it, I fell on my face and heard a voice speaking" (Ezekiel 1:28). Have you noticed the common response to the presence of the Lord—to fall facedown in worship? Don't be surprised to discover your heart moved often to worship and adore God as you learn more about Him. Following this vision, the Lord then spoke to Ezekiel. Read Ezekiel 2:1-4 and describe what God was asking of Ezekiel.

2. Throughout his lifetime, Ezekiel was given many visions, and his final vision was of the holy and heavenly city, the new Jerusalem. What hope and consolation this must have brought to the captives in Babylon! Read Ezekiel 48:35 and describe what you learn about the city.

3. *Yahweh Shammah* is translated "The LORD is there" and speaks to Yahweh's eternal presence. *The New American Commentary* describes the implications of this name:

> This name embodies the idea of the eternal residence of God with his people and the assurance that he will never again depart. Also his presence will no longer be confined to the holy of holies in the sanctuary, but he will dwell in the city whose name preserved the promise, "The Lord is there!"[7]

In Ezekiel 43:5 we see a description of God's presence—His glory—coming back into the temple. We are told, "Behold, the glory of the God of Israel was coming from the way of the east. And His voice was like the sound of many waters; and the earth shone with His glory...the glory of the LORD filled the house...He said to me, 'Son of man, this is the place of My throne and the place of the soles of My feet, where I will dwell among the sons of Israel forever'" (Ezekiel 43:2,5,7).

The name *Yahweh Shammah* speaks of the glorious presence of God Himself. In fact, through the indwelling Holy Spirit, we may even now experience His glorious presence, for He dwells in us. Just think—our hearts are His home, where the soles of His feet now tread. Read the following verses and underline the phrases and words that are most significant to you today:

> "Jesus answered him, 'If anyone really loves me, he will observe my teaching, and my Father will love him, and both of us will come in face-to-face fellowship with him; yes, we will make our special dwelling place with him'" (John 14:23 WILLIAMS).

"But all of us who are Christians have no veils on our faces, but reflect like mirrors the glory of the Lord. We are transfigured in ever-increasing splendour into his own image, and the transformation comes from the Lord who is the Spirit" (2 Corinthians 3:18 PHILLIPS).

"For God, who said, 'Let light shine out of darkness,' is the One who has shone in my heart, to give me the light of the knowledge of God's glory, reflected on the face of Christ. But I am keeping this jewel in an earthen jar, to prove that its surpassing power is God's, not mine" (2 Corinthians 4:6-7 WILLIAMS).

"For we are the temple of the living God; just as God said, 'I will dwell in them and walk among them; and I will be their God, and they shall be My people'" (2 Corinthians 6:16).

"Are you not conscious that you are God's temple, and that the Spirit of God has His permanent home in you?" (1 Corinthians 3:16 WILLIAMS).

"God has said, 'Never will I leave you, never will I forsake you'" (Hebrews 13:5 NIV).

ADORE GOD IN PRAYER

May I love you, my God and Father, with a holy, absorbing, and increasing love, not for what you give, but for who you are.[8]

F.B. MEYER

YIELD YOURSELF TO GOD

Think about these words by Herbert Lockyer regarding the name *Yahweh Shammah*:

The uniqueness and glory of Israel's faith as contrasted with the religious beliefs of surrounding idol-worshiping nations, was the presence of a holy God dwelling in the midst and the assurance of the continuation of divine Presence as they remained faithful to the covenant to be a holy people obeying a holy God...

While He made the Tabernacle, Temple, and city of old His abode, giving to Israel visible manifestations of His Presence, all that is implied by this name was not exhausted in any earthly habitation...No matter where we may go by choice or compulsion, we can never journey to any place He cannot reach...

The continuous experience of those saints whose lives are full, either of constant movement or of a fixed abode, is that of the sense of the guiding and guarding Presence of Jehovah. Brother Lawrence, amid the menial tasks of the monastery kitchen could practice, "the presence of God." David Livingstone, the famous missionary-explorer took as his motto the promise of Jesus, "Lo, I am with you always even unto the end of the world"…

What strength we have for the trials of life as we remember that as we pass through the rivers and walk in the fire we have His promise, "I will be with thee" (Isaiah 43:2)…"The Lord is there" is a privilege and a blessing to be realized by each separate believer in his own spiritual experience…May each of us be found living for God in such a Christ-exalting way that those around will be forced to say, "Surely God is in that life!" May ours be the ever-expanding vision and experience of Him as our personal *Jehovah-Shammah!*[9]

ENJOY HIS PRESENCE

Perhaps as you realize the very presence of Yahweh Shammah, knowing and understanding in a new way that He makes His home in you, you are compelled to say along with Jacob, "Surely the Lord is in this place, and I did not know it…How awesome is this place!" (Genesis 28:16-17). Oh, what an exciting day it is when you realize the truth of Paul's words in Colossians 1:27: "Christ in you, the hope of glory." He not only lives with you but also lives *in* you. If you have received Christ into your life, your heart is Christ's home.

May His presence bring times of refreshing into your life today (Acts 3:19). And finally, may His presence in you make a bold statement to the world of who resides within, the Lord Himself. Talk with Yahweh Shammah now about how much you love Him and all that He means to you today.

REST IN HIS LOVE

"God has said, 'Never will I leave you, never will I forsake you'" (Hebrews 13:5 NIV).

TRUSTING IN EL ELYON, GOD MOST HIGH

Recognize that the Most High is ruler over the realm of mankind and bestows it on whomever He wishes.

DANIEL 4:25

PREPARE YOUR HEART

Have you ever felt as though things in life were completely out of control? Has your life ever gone in a completely unexplainable direction, causing a devastating disappointment or the dashing of a dream? If so, you need to know and trust in *El Elyon*, "God Most High." Trusting in El Elyon gives you the security of knowing that God is sovereign and perfectly in control. What seems like a devastating turn of events may be understood as a bend in the road, taking you in a direction that ultimately, because of the sovereign hand of El Elyon, will lead to God's glory. Man's actions always play into the hands of El Elyon.

Daniel knew El Elyon well. In fact, the name *El Elyon* is found in the book of Daniel at least ten times. The sovereignty of God is a major theme of the book of Daniel and the focus in all the events he describes. And the sovereignty of God will become a major theme of your life when you discover, draw near to, declare, depend on, and delight in El Elyon. Ask God to speak to you today as you draw near to Him.

READ AND STUDY GOD'S WORD

1. Daniel, at the age of 15, was taken captive and exiled to Babylon. His prophecies began and ended in Babylon. He lived as an alien in a foreign land, but his real home was in God Himself. A.C. Gaebelein describes Daniel: "What faithfulness is exhibited in his life. His dependence on God, his deep piety and humility are mentioned in nearly every chapter of the Book. He was a great man of prayer."[10] The angel Gabriel told Daniel that he was "very precious to God" (Daniel 9:23 NLT).

Daniel knew many names of God, including God of heaven (Daniel 2:18), God of gods and Lord of kings (2:47), the living God (6:20), the Ancient of Days (7:9), and Commander of the host (8:11).

But one of the most repeated names was *El Elyon,* meaning "elevated, high, exalted" and stressing the absolute superiority of God. Even Nebuchadnezzar, ruler of Babylon, arrived at the conclusion that "the Most High God is ruler over the realm of mankind," and "He sets over it whomever He wishes" (Daniel 5:21).

Nebuchadnezzar had a dream he did not understand, and he called on Daniel to interpret it. Read Daniel 4:24-25 and record what you learn about the Most High God and our response to Him.

2. Daniel served during the reigns of Nebuchadnezzar and Darius (see Daniel 6:1). Daniel was such a man of integrity that the commissioners who served alongside him became jealous and devised a plan to get rid of him. They convinced Darius to make a law that anyone who prayed to a god or man besides Darius would be thrown into the lion's den. Darius foolishly signed the law. Still, Daniel "continued kneeling on his knees three times a day, praying and giving thanks before his God, as he had been doing previously" (Daniel 6:10). King Darius was distressed to discover that because his law could not be revoked, Daniel would be thrown into the lion's den. He had no choice but to follow his own decree, and yet he was confident that somehow Daniel's God would deliver him.

The next day Darius quickly rushed to the lion's den and called out to Daniel, "Daniel, servant of the living God, has your God, whom you constantly serve, been able to deliver you from the lions?" (Daniel 6:20). Read Daniel 6:21-23 to discover the rest of this true story. Then write your own observations about Daniel's character and the sovereign hand of God in the affairs of his life.

3. Often the events that perplex the minds and hearts of men are, in fact, bringing about the very plans and purposes of God. We see a case in point in the early life of Joseph, who was sold into slavery by his jealous brothers. As if that injustice were not enough, he then was wrongly imprisoned because of a false accusation from the wife of his master, Potiphar. And yet, throughout his story, we see the hand of El Elyon confidently working out His plan so that one day Joseph would become the most powerful man in Egypt, second only to the Pharaoh. Read the following verses and record what you learn about how God worked out His sovereign plan in Joseph's life:

Genesis 39:2-4

Genesis 39:21-23

Genesis 45:1-9

Genesis 50:18-21

4. Read the following verses and write your insights about the sovereign control of God in your life. Personalize what you learn from each verse:

1 Chronicles 29:11-12

Romans 8:28

ADORE GOD IN PRAYER

Take some time now and talk with El Elyon about the events of your life. Devote a prayer page in the back of this book to those circumstances in your life that are distressing you or discouraging you. Acknowledge that El Elyon is sovereign and ask Him for His help and guidance in your life. Then watch with HOPE (Holding On with Patient Expectation) as God weaves the threads of your life into His master design.

YIELD YOURSELF TO GOD

Reflect on these words by H.L. Ellison:

> We may be sure that the chief purpose of Daniel today is to bring strength and comfort to the individual or church faced by apparently overwhelming and irresistible difficulties and opposition. Its picture of God's absolute sovereignty in the crisis of the present and in the yet unveiled future is a guarantee of God's succour for all who trust Him and of His ultimate and complete triumph.[11]

ENJOY HIS PRESENCE

How do you need the comfort and assurance of El Elyon, the Most High God, today? Where do you need the confidence that God is sovereign and in control? Close your time with the Lord by writing a prayer, expressing all that is on your heart.

REST IN HIS LOVE

"Yours, O LORD, is the greatness and the power and the glory and the victory and the majesty, indeed everything that is in the heavens and the earth; Yours is the dominion, O LORD, and You exalt Yourself as head over all. Both riches and honor come from You, and You rule over all, and in Your hand is power and might; and it lies in Your hand to make great and to strengthen everyone" (1 Chronicles 29:11-12).

TRUSTING IN YAHWEH SABAOTH, THE LORD OF HOSTS

Therefore say to them, "Thus says the LORD of hosts, 'Return to Me,' declares the LORD of hosts, 'that I may return to you,' says the LORD of hosts."

ZECHARIAH 1:3

PREPARE YOUR HEART

Oh, what a day it was when Corrie ten Boom was released from Ravensbruck concentration camp. History says her release occurred due to a clerical error, but the Bible tells us that God is a "God of deliverances" (Psalm 68:20). When Paul and Silas were beaten and imprisoned for their faith, they began praying and singing hymns of praise to the Lord. While all the other prisoners were listening to them, suddenly there was an earthquake, the doors were opened, and everyone's chains were unfastened (Acts 16:25-26). No amount of earthly power is greater than the power and authority of God Himself. Today you are going to learn that God is Yahweh Sabaoth, the Lord of Hosts. He is the one you need to run to in your impossible situations for help and deliverance. He is the one who can defeat any giants you face in your life.

Prepare your heart today by reading Psalm 3 and ask the Lord to speak to you in His Word.

READ AND STUDY GOD'S WORD

1. *Yahweh Sabaoth* ("the Lord of Hosts") is found 250 times in the Old Testament and, interestingly, 173 times in the prophets (60 times each in Isaiah and Jeremiah and 53 times in Zechariah). Yahweh Sabaoth is commander of the armies of heaven (the angels) and the ruler over all power and might in both heaven and earth. When you think of the name *Yahweh Sabaoth,* think of the power, help, and deliverance of God.

The constant presence of the name *Yahweh Sabaoth* throughout Zechariah's prophecies is by God's design and purpose. Zechariah was a postexilic prophet focusing on the deliverance from the Babylonian captivity and pointing to an even greater salvation and restoration through the coming Messiah. Read the following verses in Zechariah and write out what you learn about the message and the heart of Yahweh Sabaoth, the Lord of Hosts:

Zechariah 1:3

Zechariah 1:14-17

Zechariah 3:9

Zechariah 8:2-8

2. The words of Zechariah point to a future deliverance by Messiah. Look at the following verses and write what you learn about Jesus:

Matthew 1:21

Matthew 26:51-53

John 1:29

Romans 5:6-9

Hebrews 7:25

3. Jesus paid the penalty for your sin and accomplished your deliverance. You can know that there is no one greater than Yahweh Sabaoth, commander of the armies of heaven. You can say along with Jeremiah, "the LORD is with me like a dread champion" (Jeremiah 20:11). Yahweh Sabaoth will fight the battle and defeat the giants in your life. David, the man after God's own heart, knew Yahweh Sabaoth and saw Him fight many battles, including the fight against Goliath the giant.

Read 1 Samuel 17:41-51 and describe what happened because David fought against Goliath, the Philistine, in the name of the Lord of hosts.

ADORE GOD IN PRAYER

Lift me up, by your strong arm, above the mists and darkness of the valley, to stand and walk with you on the high level of your presence and glory.[12]

F.B. MEYER

YIELD YOURSELF TO GOD

Think about these words from Alan Redpath:

David was strengthened by experience: he could look back upon a day when he slew a lion and a bear. The confidence you may have as you go out in the name of the Lord today is that in the pages of your memory you can find days when you have faced a situation that was absolutely impossible, and the Lord stepped in and gave victory. It isn't the first time you have stood against a Goliath—you know what it is to be strengthened by experience and sustained by the Word of God. So many Christians believe in the God of history and the God of prophecy; we believe all the great things He did in Wesley's day and in Moody's day. We believe in the great things He is going to do when He comes again. But how few of His people really believe that He is the God of today, that He is a present, living power in our hearts! In Saul's mind, God was absent from the whole conflict; He didn't enter into it. But in David's mind, God was the greatest reality of all.[13]

ENJOY HIS PRESENCE

What giants are you facing in your life today? Do you have impossible situations where you need deliverance? Draw near to Yahweh Sabaoth, the Lord of Hosts; pray for His strength, and ask Him to fight the battles you face today. Close your quiet time by writing a prayer on the journal pages in the back of this book.

REST IN HIS LOVE

"You shall call His name Jesus, for He will save His people from their sins" (Matthew 1:21).

DEVOTIONAL READING
BY J. I. PACKER

What were we made for? To know God. What aim should we set ourselves in life? To know God. What is the "eternal life" that Jesus gives? Knowledge of God. "This is life eternal, that they might know thee, the only true God, and Jesus Christ, whom thou hast sent" (John 17:3). What is the best thing in life, bringing more joy, delight, and contentment, than anything else? Knowledge of God. "Thus saith the LORD, let not the wise man glory in his wisdom, neither let the mighty man glory in his might, let not the rich man glory in his riches; but let him that glorieth glory in this, that he understand and knoweth me" (Jer. 9:23f.). What, of all the states God ever sees man in, gives Him most pleasure? Knowledge of Himself. "I desired...the knowledge of God more than burnt offerings," says God (Hos. 6:6)...

What we have said provides at once a foundation, shape, and goal for our lives, plus a principle of priorities, and a scale of values. Once you become aware that the main business that you are here for is to know God, most of life's problems fall into place of their own accord.[14]

Take some time now to write about all that you have learned this week. What has been most significant to you? Close by writing a prayer to the Lord.

BEHOLD HIS BEAUTY WITH JESUS, THE SON OF GOD

Thankfully, the gospel of Christ tells us how to find God, to respond to Him, to love Him. The gospel tells us that there is a door—only one door. Jesus Christ is that door, and through Him we meet God...Men and women who have met God and have chosen to live for Him have found the heavens opened...And you. If you have never met God in such an experience, He waits to grant you an encounter with Himself.

A.W. TOZER

HE HAS EXPLAINED HIM

No one has seen God at any time; the only begotten God who is
in the bosom of the Father, He has explained Him.

JOHN 1:18

PREPARE YOUR HEART

One day Jesus was talking with His disciples about heaven. During their conversation, Philip said, "Lord, show us the Father and that will be enough for us." Jesus answered, "Don't you know me, Philip, even after I have been among you such a long time? Anyone who has seen me has seen the Father" (John 14:8-9 NIV). In this dramatic exchange, Philip is looking into the eyes of God Himself. Philip wants to see God. And Jesus is saying God is with him right now. And the question He is asking Philip is one for you to consider: "Don't you know me?" This is the encouragement from Jesus: Know Me. And then you will realize you have seen the Lord.

The deity of Christ is a profound truth to realize and comprehend. He is who He claimed to be—God incarnate. What does that really mean? If you want to know what God is like, look at Jesus, for John tells us that Jesus is the explanation of God (John 1:18). The feet of God Himself trod the earth for all of mankind to watch and contemplate and comprehend. The Gospels (Matthew, Mark, Luke, and John) include numerous instances when Jesus clearly claimed to be God. He forgave sins (Matthew 9:2), healed the blind (Matthew 9:27-30), fed five thousand people (Matthew 14:21), raised Lazarus from the dead (John 11:38-44), claimed to give eternal life (John 10:28-31), and so much more. The Gospels show that the religious Jews clearly understood His claims. They said, "You, being a man, make yourself out to be God" (John 10:33). They tore their robes. They picked up stones to throw at Him. Others marveled—and believed.

As you draw near to God today in your quiet time, who do you say Jesus is? Do you realize that He is God? Do you know Him as He really is—Immanuel, God with us (Matthew 1:23)? Ask God to speak to you as you live in His Word and think about these great and powerful truths.

READ AND STUDY GOD'S WORD

1. John, a disciple of Christ, wrote his Gospel so that "you may believe that Jesus is the Christ, the Son of God; and that believing you may have life in His name" (John 20:31). Begin your time in the Word today by reading John 1:1-18. Write out everything you learn about Christ.

2. The theme of the book of Hebrews is the supremacy of Jesus Christ. The first three verses reveal a very powerful truth about Christ, one you will never want to forget. Read Hebrews 1:1-3 and record everything you learn about Christ.

3. Summarize why knowing Christ helps us understand the character and attributes of God.

ADORE GOD IN PRAYER

You have said, O Lord Jesus, that anyone who believes in you has everlasting life. I do now believe. With my whole heart I look to you as Savior, Friend, and King; and in this glad hour I receive from your hand not only life, but life more abundantly.[1]

F.B. MEYER

YIELD YOURSELF TO GOD

The first question put by Jesus to Philip, "Hast thou not known me?" was something more than a logical artifice to make stupid disciples reflect on the contents of the knowledge they already possessed. It hinted at a real fact. The disciples had really not yet *seen* Jesus, for as long as they had been with Him. They knew Him, and they did not know Him: they knew not *that* they knew, nor *what* they knew. They were like children, who can repeat the Catechism without understanding its sense, or who possess a treasure without being capable of estimating its value. They were like men looking at an object through a telescope without adjusting the focus… They had no clear, full, consistent, spiritual conception of the mind, heart, and character of the man Christ Jesus, in whom dwelt all the fulness of Godhead bodily. Nor would they possess such a conception till the Spirit of Truth, the promised Comforter, came. The very thing He was to do for them was to show them Christ; not merely to recall to their memories the details of His life, but to show them the one mind and spirit which dwelt amid the details, as the soul dwells in the body, and made them an organic whole, and which once perceived, would of itself recall to recollection all the isolated particulars at present lying latent in their consciousness. When the apostles had got that conception, they would know Christ indeed, the same Christ whom they had known before, yet different, a new Christ, because a Christ comprehended—seen with the eye of the spirit, as the former had been seen with the eye of the flesh. And when they had thus seen Christ, they would feel that they had also seen the Father. The knowledge of Christ would satisfy them, because in Him they should see with unveiled face the glory of the Lord.[2]

A.B. BRUCE

Can any rational mind, fairly considering all we have seen, continue to doubt that the appearance of Jesus Christ in this world is the most important, the central, the all-determining fact in human history? His influence has been at the heart of the greatest of civilizations, and, judging even by terrestrial analogies, that influence must ultimately remold humanity, working out the virus of sin and brightening away the blight of sorrow…

He has come: the Revealer of the snares and chasms that lurk in darkness; the Rebuker of every evil thing that prowls by night; the Stiller of the storm-winds of passion; the Quickener of all that is wholesome; the Adorner of all that is beautiful; the Reconciler of contradictions; the Harmonizer of discords; the Healer of diseases; the Savior from sin. He has come: the Torch of truth, the Anchor of hope, the Pillar of faith, the Rock for strength, the Refuge for security, the Fountain for refreshment, the Vine for gladness, the Rose for beauty, the Lamb for tenderness, the Friend for counsel, the Brother for love. Jesus Christ has trod the world. The trace of the Divine footsteps will never be obliterated…

Let us deliberately crown Him Lord of all. In practice and in speculation, in intellect and in affection, in the family circle, in the social throng, in the political enterprise, in the inmost recesses of our being, in the slightest outgoing of our activity, let Him reign perpetually, unreservedly, supremely![3]

PETER BAYNE

ENJOY HIS PRESENCE

What do you say to the claims of Christ? Jesus asked His disciples, "But who do you say that I am?" (Matthew 16:15). Simon Peter answered, "You are the Christ, the Son of the Living God." Peter Bayne, in his book *The Testimony of Christ to Christianity,* responded similarly when he said, "He was the Messiah of God; and…whatsoever He said was true and authoritative." If Jesus were to ask you today, "Who do you say that I am?" how would you respond? Conclude your quiet time today by summarizing in two or three sentences your thoughts about Jesus Christ—who He is and what He means to you.

REST IN HIS LOVE

"He is the radiance of His glory and the exact representation of His nature, and upholds all things by the word of His power. When He had made purification of sins, He sat down at the right hand of the Majesty on high" (Hebrews 1:3).

THE ETERNAL I AM

Jesus said to them, "Truly, truly, I say to you, before Abraham was born, I am."
JOHN 8:58

PREPARE YOUR HEART

Imagine you are in Nazareth during the time of Jesus. You are sitting in the synagogue on the Sabbath. A man named Jesus walks into the synagogue and is invited to read. Someone hands Jesus the scroll of Isaiah, and He opens it to a specific place—Isaiah 61. He reads, "The Spirit of the LORD is upon Me, because He anointed Me to preach the gospel to the poor. He has sent Me to proclaim release to the captives, and recovery of sight to the blind, to set free those who are oppressed, to proclaim the favorable year of the Lord." Everyone knows that this passage of Scripture clearly speaks of the coming Messiah, promised by Yahweh. Then Jesus closes the book, hands it back to the attendant, and sits down. Every eye is fixed on Jesus. Then He says the most astounding words of all: "Today this Scripture has been fulfilled in your hearing" (Luke 4:21).

Make no mistake. Jesus was clear about who He was. He proclaimed His identity to all who would listen. Had you been living on the earth during the time of Jesus, you might have been in the crowd and heard what He said. If so, you would have been moved to respond to Him because He always commanded a response.

The wonderful truth is that you have His Word, the Bible, and you can respond to Him even today. May His words bring you to a deep faith, trust, and love for Him.

READ AND STUDY GOD'S WORD

1. Wherever Jesus went, discussions and even arguments arose about who He was. But never was the exchange quite so heated as the day Jesus talked about Yahweh with the religious Jews. In a discussion with the Pharisees who were challenging Jesus' identity, Jesus said, "Truly, truly, I say to you, before Abraham was born, I am" (John 8:58). You have studied the name *I AM* and already are familiar with the word *Yahweh*. But just imagine the impact when Jesus said He was Yahweh! He was clearly claiming to be God. The response of the Jews showed that they understood His claims: "Therefore they picked up stones to throw at Him, but Jesus hid Himself and went

out of the temple" (John 8:59). Here's the powerful truth for you to think about today: Yahweh was standing in their midst. He walked on this earth. He is the great I AM.

Read John 8:56-59 and write out your most significant insights regarding what Jesus said about Himself.

---

2. Jesus made a number of statements about Himself, revealing in a new way the multifaceted nature of I AM. Look at the following verses and write out what you learn about Jesus as the I AM.

John 6:35

John 8:12

John 10:7-9

John 10:11,14

John 11:25

John 14:6

John 15:1,5

3. Jesus is clearly claiming to be Yahweh, the one who is everything you need for every circumstance of life. As bread, He is your sustenance and will sustain you through every difficulty. As light, He brings growth and brightens every darkness. As the door, He provides the way to eternal life. As the shepherd, He gives security, provision, and comfort. As the resurrection and the life, He gives you eternal life. As the way, the truth, and the life, He provides the standard, the only true measure of life. As the vine, He is the resource for your every need. Take some time now to think about these great truths you've learned in the Word of God and summarize in two or three sentences what is most important to you today. How does what you have seen in Jesus shed light on all you have learned about Yahweh in this quiet time experience?

ADORE GOD IN PRAYER

Thou Great I AM,
Fill my mind with elevation and grandeur at the thought of a Being
with whom one day is as a thousand years,
and a thousand years as one day,
a mighty God who, amidst the lapse of worlds,
and the revolutions of empires,
feels no variableness,
but is glorious in immortality.
May I rejoice that, while men die, the Lord lives;
that, while all creatures are broken reeds,
empty cisterns,
fading flowers,
withering grass,
he is the rock of ages, the fountain of living waters.
Turn my heart from vanity,
from dissatisfactions,
from uncertainties of the present state,
to an eternal interest in Christ.
Let me remember that life is short and unforeseen,
and is only an opportunity for usefulness;
give me a holy avarice to redeem the time,

to awake at every call to charity and piety,
so that I may feed the hungry,
clothe the naked,
instruct the ignorant,
reclaim the vicious,
forgive the offender,
diffuse the gospel,
show neighbourly love to all.
Let me live a life of self-distrust,
dependence on thyself,
mortification,
crucifixion,
prayer.[4]

YIELD YOURSELF TO GOD

Reflect on these words by James Montgomery Boice:

Practically everything that Jesus had to say was an indirect claim to divinity…he claimed to be all that men need for a full spiritual life. Only God can rightly make such claims. "I am the bread of life" (John 6:35). "I am the light of the world" (8:12; 9:5). "I am the gate" (10:7,9). "I am the good shepherd" (10:11,14). "I am the resurrection and the life" (11:25). "I am the way and the truth and the life" (14:6). "I am the true vine" (15:1,5).

One great and final example of Christ's unique conception of himself occurred shortly after the resurrection on the day Jesus appeared among the disciples, Thomas being present. Jesus had appeared to the disciples earlier when Thomas was absent. But when Thomas was told about the appearance, he had replied, "Unless I see the nail marks in his hands and put my finger where the nails were, and put my hand into his side, I will not believe it" (20:25). Now the Lord appeared to them all once more, this time including Thomas, and he asked Thomas to make the test he had wanted to make: "Put your finger here…and reach out your hand" (v. 27). Thomas, who was overcome by Christ's presence, immediately fell to the ground and worshiped him saying, "My Lord and my God" (v. 28). Think of it: "Lord and God!" *Adonai! Elohim! Jehovah!* And Jesus accepted the designation! He did not deny it! It is no wonder, in light of this testimony, that this is the story John chooses to end all but the postscript of his Gospel.

These, then, are a few of Christ's claims. Thus, whatever we may think of the claims themselves, there can at least be no doubt that Christ made them. Moreover, they remain unchanged. History has not eradicated Christ's claim to be God. Time has not changed it. The Jesus who made the claim then is the same Jesus who is our living contemporary, and the Scriptures tell us that he is the same "yesterday and today and forever." He calls on you to follow him. Will you do it, forsaking all else? If he is not God, then you can safely ignore him. But if he is God, then anything less than a total surrender to him is folly and any other loyalty is idolatrous.[5]

ENJOY HIS PRESENCE

As you close your quiet time, think about all the I AM statements made by Christ in the book of John. Where is your need today? Will you draw near to Him, thanking Him for who He is and asking Him to meet you in the depth of your own need? You can trust Him as the eternal I AM—Yahweh. He is everything you need for every circumstance of life.

REST IN HIS LOVE

"I am the Light of the world; he who follows Me will not walk in the darkness, but will have the Light of life" (John 8:12).

THE BEAUTY OF THE LORD

Come to Me, all who are weary and heavy-laden, and I will give you rest. Take
My yoke upon you and learn from Me, for I am gentle and humble in heart, and
you will find rest for your souls. For My yoke is easy and My burden is light.
MATTHEW 11:28-30

PREPARE YOUR HEART

There are profound experiences in your life journey when you realize in new ways the beautiful character of your Lord—His love, His joy, His peace. Brennan Manning, author and priest, describes the day he realized the love of Jesus Christ as an experience of bewildering strength and feeling, as though a hand gripped his heart.

> I could barely breathe. It was abrupt and startling. The awareness of being loved was no longer gentle, tender and comfortable. The love of Christ, the crucified Son of God, for me, took on the wildness, passion, and fury of a sudden spring storm. Like a bursting dam, spasms of convulsive crying erupted from the depths of my being. He died on the Cross for me! I had known that before, but in the way that Cardinal Newman describes as notional knowledge—abstract, far away, largely irrelevant to the gut issues of life, just another trinket in the dusty pawnshop of dogmatic beliefs. But in one blinding moment of salvific truth, it was real knowledge calling for personal engagement of my mind and heart. Christianity was no longer simply a moral code but a love affair, the thrill, the excitement, the incredible, passionate joy of being loved and falling in love with Jesus Christ.[6]

Jesus shows us the heart of God. He is the true explanation of God. No time is ever wasted gazing at the beauty of Christ, for each second spent looking at Him affords a deeper intimacy with God. Ask the Lord now to open your eyes that you might behold His beauty.

READ AND STUDY GOD'S WORD

1. The Gospel accounts of Jesus reveal His humble and tender heart. This gentle tenderness Jesus displays, showing us what God is like, is absolutely astounding. No human could ever guess

this truth about God unless God Himself had revealed it. We see glimpses of His tender and unabashed love for us when He makes statements in the Old Testament such as these:

> "Here am I, here am I. I have spread out My hands all day long to a rebellious people" (Isaiah 65:1-2).

> "I thought, 'After she has done all these things she will return to Me' but she did not return" (Jeremiah 3:7).

> "I have loved you with an everlasting love; therefore I have drawn you with lovingkindness" (Jeremiah 31:3).

In these few examples from God's Word, you see God's incredible desire, humility, tenderness, and love. You see His invitation to us.

When you discover the open heart of God, you cannot help but run into His arms. His invitation is apparent in the words of Jesus, especially in Matthew 11:28-30. Look at these verses in the following translations and underline your favorite words and phrases:

> "Come to Me, all who are weary and heavy-laden, and I will give you rest. Take My yoke upon you and learn from Me, for I am gentle and humble in heart, and you will find rest for your souls. For my yoke is easy and My burden is light."

> "Come to me, all of you who are tired and have heavy loads, and I will give you rest. Accept my teachings and learn from me, because I am gentle and humble in spirit, and you will find rest for your lives. The teaching that I ask you to accept is easy; the load I give you to carry is light" (NCV).

> "Then Jesus said, 'Come to me, all of you who are weary and carry heavy burdens, and I will give you rest. Take my yoke upon you. Let me teach you, because I am humble and gentle at heart, and you will find rest for your souls. For my yoke is easy to bear, and the burden I give you is light'" (NLT).

> "Are you tired? Worn out? Burned out on religion? Come to me. Get away with me and you'll recover your life. I'll show you how to take a real rest. Walk with me and work with me—watch how I do it. Learn the unforced rhythms of grace. I won't lay anything heavy or ill-fitting on you. Keep company with me and you'll learn to live freely and lightly" (MSG).

2. Look at the following verses and record what you learn about the Lord:

Luke 1:78

John 3:16

John 10:11-15

John 11:35

Philippians 2:5-8

Titus 3:4-7

ADORE GOD IN PRAYER

Use the words of this beloved hymn written by Louisa M.R. Stead to worship the Lord today:

> 'Tis so sweet to trust in Jesus,
> Just to take Him at His Word;
> Just to rest upon His promise,
> Just to know, "Thus says the Lord."
>
> Oh, how sweet to trust in Jesus,
> Just to trust His cleansing blood;
> Just in simple faith to plunge me
> 'Neath the healing, cleansing flood!

Yes, 'tis sweet to trust in Jesus,
Just from sin and self to cease;
Just from Jesus simply taking
Life and rest, and joy and peace.

I'm so glad I learned to trust Thee,
Precious Jesus, Savior, Friend;
And I know that Thou art with me,
Wilt be with me to the end.

Jesus, Jesus, how I trust Him!
How I've proved Him o'er and o'er!
Jesus, Jesus, precious Jesus!
O for grace to trust Him more!

YIELD YOURSELF TO GOD

By giving himself up to death, the incarnate God demonstrated the full depths of his love for mankind. It is indeed the love *of God* which we are dealing with, in that it is none other than God himself who loved us and gave himself for us.[7]

ALISTAIR McGRATH

His glory lay in the fact that He was perfect love in a loveless world; that He was perfect purity in an impure world; that He was perfect meekness in a harsh and quarrelsome world. There was no end to His glory. He was perfect humility in a world where every man was seeking his own benefit. He was boundless and fathomless mercy in a hard and cruel world where every man was seeking his own benefit. He was completely selfless goodness in a world full of selfishness.[8]

A.W. TOZER

What other happiness can lift your soul so much as this—to know that He who is highest, fairest, noblest, and most honored is also the lowest and humblest? He is so full of regal courtesy toward us, whom He accepts as brothers and sisters![9]

JULIAN OF NORWICH

ENJOY HIS PRESENCE

What is the most important truth you have learned about your Lord today? What is your response to Him? How can you trust Him today? Close by writing a prayer to Him, expressing all that is on your heart.

REST IN HIS LOVE

"I am the good shepherd, and I know My own and My own know Me, even as the Father knows Me and I know the Father; and I lay down My life for the sheep" (John 10:14-15).

INTIMATE COMMUNION

But Jesus Himself would often slip away to the wilderness and pray.
LUKE 5:16

PREPARE YOUR HEART

When you open the pages of your Bible and read the detailed events of Jesus' life, you will learn much from His example. And one quality stands out in His life—He enjoyed intimate communion with His Father. Jesus could have enjoyed the popularity of an adoring crowd, but instead, He chose to get alone with His Father in the wilderness. His constant withdrawing to the quiet desert places, even though His time on earth was short, bids us to do the same. Ask the Lord today to show you through His example how to find a quiet place and enjoy intimate communion with Him. Begin your quiet time today by communing with your Lord, using these words that William Featherston wrote at age 16:

My Jesus, I love Thee, I know Thou art mine;
For Thee all the follies of sin I resign.
My gracious Redeemer, my Savior art Thou;
If ever I loved Thee, my Jesus, 'tis now.

I love Thee because Thou has first loved me,
And purchased my pardon on Calvary's tree.
I love Thee for wearing the thorns on Thy brow;
If ever I loved Thee, my Jesus, 'tis now.

I'll love Thee in life, I will love Thee in death,
And praise Thee as long as Thou lendest me breath;
And say when the death dew lies cold on my brow,
If ever I loved Thee, my Jesus, 'tis now.

In mansions of glory and endless delight,
I'll ever adore Thee in heaven so bright;

I'll sing with the glittering crown on my brow;
If ever I loved Thee, my Jesus, 'tis now.

READ AND STUDY GOD'S WORD

1. Jesus' popularity grew as He continued His public ministry. He taught thousands of people, spent time with His disciples, and healed many who were suffering physical and mental afflictions. The Gospels show Jesus practicing a very important discipline of devotion. Jesus had a quiet time. Look at the following verses and record what you learn about this most important time in His day:

Mark 1:35

Luke 5:15-16

2. Once you realize Jesus spent time alone with the Father, you cannot help but wonder about His life of prayer. Jesus shared a unique intimacy with His Father, and what He knew about God His Father figured profoundly into His prayers. One day His disciples asked Him, "Lord, teach us to pray just as John also taught his disciples" (Luke 11:1). With that request, we are given a window into Jesus' prayer life. When He responded to their appeal, Jesus revealed an important truth about God, especially vital for us to remember in our own worship and delight of God. He said, "Father, hallowed be Your name."

The Greek word translated "hallowed" is *hagiazo* and means "holy, sanctified, consecrated, set apart, and pure." Jesus is teaching that God is holy. Jonathan Edwards, in contemplating the meaning of holiness, described it as "a sweet, calm, pleasant, charming, serene nature, which brought an inexpressible purity, brightness, peacefulness, ravishment to the soul…it made the soul like a field or garden of God, with all manner of pleasant fruits and flowers, all delightful and undisturbed, enjoying a sweet calm and the gentle vivifying beams of the sun."[10]

Think about the following verses about holiness and purity and underline the most significant words and phrases in each as you worship your Lord today:

"There is no one holy like the LORD, indeed there is no one besides You, nor is there any rock like our God" (1 Samuel 2:2).

"Who may ascend into the hill of the LORD? And who may stand in His holy place? He who has clean hands and a pure heart, who has not lifted up his soul to falsehood and has not sworn deceitfully. He shall receive a blessing from the LORD and righteousness from the God of his salvation. This is the generation of those who seek Him, who seek Your face" (Psalm 24:3-6).

"I shall remember the deeds of the LORD; surely I will remember Your wonders of old. I will meditate on all Your work and muse on Your deeds. Your way, O God, is holy; What god is great like our God? You are the God who works wonders; You have made known Your strength among the peoples" (Psalm 77:11-14).

"As obedient children, do not be conformed to the former lusts which were yours in your ignorance, but like the Holy One who called you, be holy yourselves also in all your behavior; because it is written, 'You shall be holy, for I am holy'" (1 Peter 1:14-16).

"What marvelous love the Father has extended to us! Just look at it—we're called children of God! That's who we really are. But that's also why the world doesn't recognize us or take us seriously, because it has no idea who he is or what he's up to. But friends, that's exactly who we are: children of God. And that's only the beginning. Who knows how we'll end up! What we know is that when Christ is openly revealed, we'll see him—and in seeing him, become like him. All of us who look forward to his Coming stay ready, with the glistening purity of Jesus' life as a model for our own" (1 John 3:1-3 MSG).

3. In another prayer of Jesus in John 17, we see a rare glimpse into the kind of conversation Jesus had with His Father. Imagine you are listening in on this most intimate communion and read John 17. Write out the verse that means the most to you.

ADORE GOD IN PRAYER

Worship your Lord and express your love and devotion to Him. You might want to use some of the verses in today's "Read and Study God's Word" section.

YIELD YOURSELF TO GOD

May not the inadequacy of much of our spiritual experience be traced back to our habit of skipping through the corridors of the Kingdom like children through the market place, chattering about everything, but pausing to learn the true value of nothing?[11]

A.W. TOZER

Of course we do not have much time! And we do not think about important things because of our 20th century noise and confusion. The devil does everything possible to keep us busy. As a result, very few of us are ever really alone with God…Very few of us know the secret of bathing our souls in silence. It was a secret our Lord Jesus Christ knew very well. There were times when He had to send the multitudes away so He could retire alone into the silence of the mountainside. There He would turn the God-ward side of His soul toward heaven.[12]

A.W. TOZER

ENJOY HIS PRESENCE

Have you learned the secret of quiet time alone with God everyday, when you gaze in wonder on the face of God and commune in silence with your Lord, who loves you? Jesus is your example, for He often withdrew to a quiet place to draw near to His Father. Take some time now to reflect on your life. How can you change your schedule to create space for your Lord each day? Close your quiet time by writing a prayer on a journal page in the back of this book, committing yourself anew to quiet time with the Lord.

REST IN HIS LOVE

"In the early morning, while it was still dark, Jesus got up, left the house, and went away to a secluded place, and was praying there" (Mark 1:35).

ABBA! FATHER!

And He was saying, "Abba! Father! All things are possible for You; remove
this cup from Me; yet not what I will, but what You will."

MARK 14:36

PREPARE YOUR HEART

What words would you use to describe your relationship with God? Do you realize the intimacy you may enjoy because of Jesus' death on the cross? When Jeanette Clift George, the actress who portrayed Corrie ten Boom in the movie *The Hiding Place,* speaks in churches, she often illustrates the intimate relationship between God and His children. She begins by setting up an area on the stage called "the Holy of Holies," representing the very dwelling place of God Himself. Only the high priest is allowed in this place. Then she marks an area just outside the veil of the Holy of Holies for the other priests. She chooses a group from the audience to represent the 12 tribes of Israel. Another group from the audience represents those in the outer courts of the temple. Finally, she chooses others to represent some of the Gentiles who may have been lingering outside the walls, hoping for any word from God.

She then explains that she would have been one of those lingering outside the walls, hoping, waiting, wishing she could be close to God. Then she describes the coming of Christ, His death on the cross, and the ripping of the temple veil from top to bottom (Matthew 27:51). As she describes what Jesus has done on the cross and the result of His death, she begins to make her way through those lingering at the temple walls and then through the outer court of the temple.

"Excuse me," she says, as she walks into the court of the temple. She then walks through the audience of priests outside the veil of the Holy of Holies. Then, she pushes aside the ripped veil, and gingerly steps inside the Holy of Holies, where God Himself dwells. She quietly but firmly tells the high priest to please leave because she and God would like to be alone. He hurries away, infuriated at the command. Then, she sits in God's presence, folds her hands in her lap, looks up with a childlike expression and says, "Hi, God. It's me, Jeanette."[13]

This story is a reminder to you that you are a child of the King. You may talk with Him anytime. The way is made clear for you to run right into His arms. Draw near to God now and ask Him to deepen your relationship with Him as you look today at a new name for God, *Abba, Father.*

READ AND STUDY GOD'S WORD

1. Jesus addressed His Father in a special, most intimate way when He was in the depth of suffering—His dark night of the soul. He was in the Garden of Gethsemane just before His arrest and crucifixion on the cross. He prayed, "Abba! Father! All things are possible for You; remove this cup from Me; yet not what I will, but what You will" (Mark 14:36). *Abba* is the Aramaic word translated "Father" and is used in the spirit of a tender, affectionate child in much the same way as a child today would use the word *daddy*. Jesus used *Father* in His prayers much more often than other Jewish teachers and writers.

Look at the following references to our Father in the New Testament and write what you learn about Him:

Matthew 6:4-8

Luke 23:34

1 Corinthians 8:5-6

Ephesians 1:3

2. Because of our new relationship with God through Christ, we may employ this display of affection, this expression of endearment, *Abba, Father.* Imagine—in addition to trusting in all the other names of God, we also have the privilege of addressing God as *Papa, Daddy, Father.* What can that mean except we have now been ushered into an even more intimate relationship with our God? According to Paul, now that we are adopted to sonship, we may call Him *Abba, Father.* Read the following two verses and underline the words and phrases most significant to you today.

> "For you have not received a spirit of slavery leading to fear again, but you have received a spirit of adoption as sons by which we cry out, 'Abba! Father!' The Spirit Himself testifies with our spirit that we are children of God, and if children, heirs

also, heirs of God and fellow heirs with Christ, if indeed we suffer with Him so that we may also be glorified with Him" (Romans 8:15-17).

"Because you are sons, God has sent forth the Spirit of His Son into our hearts, crying, 'Abba! Father!' Therefore you are no longer a slave, but a son; and if a son, then an heir through God" (Galatians 4:6-7).

ADORE GOD IN PRAYER

Will you crawl up into the lap of your Abba, Father now and lay all your cares and worries in His loving arms?

YIELD YOURSELF TO GOD

Think about the following words by A.B. Bruce:

The name [Father], in Christ's lips, always represents a definite thought, and teaches a great truth. When He uses the term to express the relation of the Invisible One to Himself, He gives us a glimpse into the mystery of the Divine Being, telling us that God is not abstract being, as Platonists and Arians conceived Him; not the absolute, incapable of relations; not a passionless being, without affections; but one who eternally loves, and is loved, in whose infinite nature the family affections find scope for ceaseless play—One in three: Father, Son, and Holy Ghost, three persons in one divine substance. Then again, when He calls God Father, in reference to mankind in general, as He does repeatedly, He proclaims to men sunk in ignorance and sin this blessed truth: "God, my Father, is your Father too; cherishes a paternal feeling towards you, though ye be so marred in moral vision that He might well not know you, and so degenerate that He might well be ashamed to own you; and I His Son am come, your elder brother, to bring you back to your Father's house. Ye are not worthy to be called His sons, for ye have ceased to bear His image, and ye have not yielded Him filial obedience and reverence; nevertheless, He is willing to be a Father unto you, and receive you graciously in His arms. Believe this, and become in heart and conduct sons of God, that ye may enjoy the full, the spiritual and eternal, benefit of God's paternal love." When, finally, He calls God Father, with special reference to His own disciples, He assures them that they are the objects of God's constant, tender, and effective care; that all His power, wisdom, and love are engaged for their protection, preservation, guidance, and final eternal salvation; that their Father in heaven will see that they lack no good, and will make all things minister to their interest, and in the end secure to them their inheritance in the everlasting kingdom. "Fear not," is His comforting message to His little chosen flock, "it is your Father's good pleasure to give you the kingdom."[14]

ENJOY HIS PRESENCE

Do you realize the great privilege of addressing God as *Abba, Father*? Spurgeon says, "If an earthly father watches over his children with unceasing love and care, how much more does our heavenly Father? Abba, Father! He who can say this, hath uttered better music than cherubim or seraphim can reach. There is heaven in the depth of that word—Father! There is all I can ask; all my necessities can demand; all my wishes can desire. I have all in all to all eternity when I can say, 'Father.'"[15] What can you learn from the example of Jesus about trusting in Abba, Father? How do you need to trust in your Father today?

REST IN HIS LOVE

"Because you are sons, God has sent forth the Spirit of His Son into our hearts, crying, 'Abba! Father!' Therefore you are no longer a slave, but a son; and if a son, then an heir through God" (Galatians 4:6-7).

DEVOTIONAL READING
BY CHARLES SPURGEON

Spiritual knowledge of Christ will be a *personal* knowledge. I cannot know Jesus through another person's acquaintance with him. No, I must know him *myself;* I must know him on my own account. It will be an *intelligent* knowledge—I must know *him,* not as the visionary dreams of him, but as the Word reveals him. I must know his natures, divine and human. I must know his offices—his attributes—his works—his shame—his glory. I must meditate upon him until I "comprehend with all saints what is the breadth, and length, and depth, and height; and know the love of Christ, which passeth knowledge." It will be an *affectionate* knowledge of him; indeed, if I know him at all, I must love him. An ounce of heart knowledge is worth a ton of head learning. Our knowledge of him will be a *satisfying* knowledge. When I know my Saviour, my mind will be full to the brim—I shall feel that I have that which my spirit panted after. "This is that bread whereof if a man eat he shall never hunger." At the same time it will be an *exciting* knowledge; the more I know of my Beloved, the more I shall want to know. The higher I climb, the loftier will be the summits which invite my eager footsteps. I shall want the more as I get the more. Like the miser's treasure, my gold will make me covet more. To conclude; this knowledge of Christ Jesus will be a most *happy* one; in fact, so elevating, that sometimes it will completely bear me up above all trials, and doubts, and sorrows; and it will, while I enjoy it, make me something more than "Man that is born of woman, who is of few days, and full of trouble"; for it will fling about me the immortality of the ever living Saviour, and gird me with the golden girdle of his eternal joy. Come, my soul, sit at Jesus' feet and learn of him all this day.[16]

Take some time now to write about all that you have learned this week. What has been most significant to you? Close by writing a prayer to the Lord.

BEHOLD HIS BEAUTY WITH THE DISCIPLES WHO WALKED WITH GOD

Untried, untrodden, and unknown as your future path may be, it is, each step, mapped, arranged, and provided for in the everlasting and unchangeable covenant of God. To Him who leads us, who accepts us in the Son of His love, who knows the end from the beginning, it is no new, or uncertain, or hidden way. We thank Him that while He wisely and kindly veils all the future from our reach, all that future—its minutest event—is as transparent and visible to Him as the past. Our Shepherd knows the windings along which He skillfully, gently, and safely leads His flock. He has traveled that way Himself, and has left the traces of His presence on the road. And as each follower advances—the new path unfolding at each step—he can exultingly exclaim, "I see the footprint of my Lord; here went my Master, my Leader, my Captain, leaving me an example that I should follow His steps."

OCTAVIUS WINSLOW

WHEN YOU SEE HIS GLORY

And He was transfigured before them; and His face shone like the sun, and His garments became as white as light.

MATTHEW 17:2

PREPARE YOUR HEART

It is fitting that we end our journey by walking this week with the disciples and catching a glimpse of what they saw and learned about God. We who have answered the call to follow Jesus Christ are His disciples too. Oh, what a day it must have been when each of the disciples met Jesus for the first time. Their lives were changed forever. Their experience is your experience, for no one who meets the God of gods, King of kings, and Lord of lords is left untouched. Describing his own experience, John said, "We saw His glory" (John 1:14). The light of His glory will change the countenance of your face. Will you draw near to Him now and pray the prayer of Moses? *Lord, please, show me Your glory* (Exodus 33:18 NKJV).

READ AND STUDY GOD'S WORD

1. Last week we saw that Jesus is the explanation of God (John 1:18), the radiance of His glory, and the exact representation of His nature (Hebrews 1:3). Imagine the incredible privilege those original disciples enjoyed as they walked with Jesus. A.B. Bruce, in his book *The Training of the Twelve,* describes their firsthand experience as "eye and ear witnessing of an unparalleled life."[1] One of their greatest experiences with Jesus occurred when Jesus took Peter, James, and John up on a high mountain. Imagine being all alone with the King of kings and Lord of Lords on the top of a mountain! Read Matthew 17:1-8 and describe what these disciples experienced, including what they heard and what they saw.

195

2. Peter, James, and John saw Jesus transfigured before their eyes and caught just a glimpse of the glory of God as they saw His radiance, heard the voice of God, and even saw Elijah and Moses keeping company with Jesus. Another disciple of the Lord, Stephen, was also granted a glimpse of the glory of God, just prior to his death. Read Acts 7:54-60 and describe what Stephen saw.

3. Wherever God is, there is His glory. And what is glory? It is the splendor and reality of His presence. In your adventure of knowing God, you are promised the experience of His glory. His Word promises it. Look at the following verses and write what you learn about the glory of God:

Romans 5:1-2

Romans 8:18

2 Corinthians 3:7-11

2 Corinthians 3:16-18

2 Corinthians 4:6

Ephesians 5:27

Revelation 21:9-11

Adore God in Prayer

O Lord Jesus Christ, give me such communion with you that my soul may continually thirst for that time when I shall behold you in your glory. In the meanwhile, may I behold your glory in the mirror of your Word and be changed into your image.[2]

F.B. Meyer

Yield Yourself to God

How great the difference between Moses and Jesus! When the prophet of Horeb had been forty days upon the mountain, he underwent a kind of transfiguration, so that his countenance shone with exceeding brightness, and he put a veil over his face, for the people could not endure to look upon his glory. Not so our Savior. He had been transfigured with a greater glory than that of Moses, and yet, it is not written that the people were blinded by the blaze of his countenance, but rather they were amazed, and running to him they saluted him (Mark 9:15). The glory of the law repels, but the greater glory of Jesus attracts. Though Jesus is holy and just, yet blended with his purity there is so much of truth and grace, that sinners run to him amazed at his goodness, fascinated by his love; they salute him, become his disciples, and take him to be their Lord and Master.[3]

Charles Spurgeon

ENJOY HIS PRESENCE

As you close your time with the Lord today, what is the most important truth you have learned about the glory of the Lord? What words would you use to describe the glory of the Lord? And finally, write out how we experience the glory of the Lord now and how we will experience the glory of God in eternity.

REST IN HIS LOVE

"And he carried me away in the Spirit to a great and high mountain, and showed me the holy city, Jerusalem, coming down out of heaven from God, having the glory of God" (Revelation 21:10-11).

WHEN YOU EXPERIENCE HIS POWER

And He said to me, "My grace is sufficient for you, for power is perfected in weakness." Most gladly, therefore, I will rather boast about my weaknesses, so that the power of Christ may dwell in me.

2 CORINTHIANS 12:9

PREPARE YOUR HEART

Francis Asbury (1745–1816) was a circuit rider who rode horseback from New England to the Carolinas and from the Atlantic to Kentucky, sharing the gospel with all who would listen. He crossed the Allegheny Mountains at least 60 times. He faced the dangers of wild animals and stalking Indians, slept on the ground with a stone for a pillow, cooked on a campfire, and battled frequent illnesses and a weak body. He used his riding time to pray and read his Bible, commentaries, or other books. And he kept a journal. He held camp meetings that became so popular that the Methodists were encouraged to hold 400 meetings of their own. Nancy Hanks, the mother of Abraham Lincoln, frequented Asbury's camp meetings. Asbury became one of the best-known people in America during his era and even preached to the House of Representatives in Washington. God used him in an influential way as he ordained more than three thousand ministers and preached more than seventeen thousand sermons. During his lifetime the Methodists grew from 1160 to 214,235 members.

What was the secret to the life of Francis Asbury? The power of God. A year before he died, he wrote, "My eyes fail...It is my fifty-fifth year of ministry and forty-fifth of labor in America...But whether health, life, or death, good is the will of the Lord; I will trust Him; yea, and will praise Him; He is the strength of my heart and my portion forever—Glory! Glory! Glory!"[4]

On your journey of trusting in the names of God, you will discover His unlimited power. God's power manifests itself in His people in unusual ways. Today you will look at the power of God at work in one of His choice servants—Paul, the apostle to the Gentiles.

READ AND STUDY GOD'S WORD

1. Paul, a religious Jew, was called by the Lord to be His witness to the Gentiles. He experienced a powerful conversion when he was met on the road to Damascus by none other than the

Lord Jesus Himself (see Acts 9:1-30). He suffered much during his life, but one challenge in particular was particularly distressful. The pain was so great that Paul begged the Lord three times to remove his "thorn in the flesh." Paul learned a very important truth about God in the crucible of his suffering.

Read 2 Corinthians 12:7-8 and record everything you learn about Paul.

Read 2 Corinthians 12:9-10 and record everything you learn about the power of God.

2. God's power is what you need in your weakness. In fact, your battle cry will become, "I can't, but He can." The Greek word translated "power" in 2 Corinthians 12 is *dunamis* and refers to a power that makes you able and capable. God gives you the ability to do what you cannot do by yourself. Look at the following verses and underline the words and phrases that help you understand the power of God in your own life.

> "The LORD is my strength and my song, and He has become my salvation" (Psalm 118:14).

> "But you will receive power when the Holy Spirit has come upon you; and you shall be My witnesses both in Jerusalem, and in all Judea and Samaria, and even to the remotest part of the earth" (Acts 1:8).

> "But we have this treasure in earthen vessels, so that the surpassing greatness of the power will be of God and not from ourselves; we are afflicted in every way, but not crushed; perplexed, but not despairing; persecuted, but not forsaken; struck down, but not destroyed" (2 Corinthians 4:7-9).

> "I pray that the eyes of your heart may be enlightened, so that you will know what is the hope of His calling, what are the riches of the glory of His inheritance in the saints, and what is the surpassing greatness of His power toward us who believe. These are in accordance with the working of the strength of His might which He brought about in Christ, when He raised Him from the dead and seated Him at His right hand in the heavenly places" (Ephesians 1:18-20).

> "I can do all things through Him who strengthens me" (Philippians 4:13).

3. Considering all you have learned today, what difference will the power of God make in your life?

ADORE GOD IN PRAYER

Pray through the words of Psalm 148 today, worshipping the Lord in all His power and glory.

YIELD YOURSELF TO GOD

Reflect on these words by John Henry Jowett:

> Here truly is a perfect equipment for life's battle, and this equipment is absolutely and entirely found in God…The first thing we need is that our weakness be transformed, and that we become possessed of resource. All other gifts are useless if this initial gift be denied. A box of tools would be impotent without the strong hand to use them…The Lord imparts unto us that primary strength of character which makes everything in the life work with intensity and decision. We are "strengthened with all might by His Spirit in the inner man." And the strength is continuous; reserves of power come to us which we cannot exhaust. "As thy days, so shall thy strength be," strength of will, strength of affection, strength of judgment, strength of ideals and of achievement. "The Lord is my strength," strength to *go on*. He gives us the power to tread the dead level, to walk the long lane that seems never to have a turning, to go through those long reaches of life which afford no pleasant surprise, and which depress the spirits in the sameness of a terrible drudgery. "The Lord is my strength," strength to *go up*. He is to me the power by which I can ascend the Hill Difficulty, and not be afraid. "They shall walk and not faint." "The Lord is my strength," strength to *go down*…It is when we leave the bracing heights, where the wind and the sun have been about us, and when we begin to come down the hill into closer and more sultry spheres, that the heart is apt to grow faint. When a man has reached his height, the height of his fame and popularity, and he begins to go down the hill, it is then he requires exceptional resource.[5]

ENJOY HIS PRESENCE

In what ways do you need to trust God for the exceptional resources of His power and strength in your life today?

REST IN HIS LOVE

"I can do all things through Him who strengthens me" (Philippians 4:13).

TRUSTING IN THE GOD OF HOPE

Now may the God of hope fill you with all joy and peace in believing, so that you will abound in hope by the power of the Holy Spirit.

ROMANS 15:13

PREPARE YOUR HEART

David Livingstone was the first missionary to take the gospel to Africa. He traveled more than 29,000 miles in Africa, discovering many parts previously unknown, including lakes Ngami, Shirwa, Malawi, and Bangweulu, the upper Zambesi and many other rivers, and the spectacular Victoria Falls.

His wife, Mary, was his beloved companion, and her death in 1862 from the African fever dealt a devastating blow to him. He experienced deep sorrow and discouragement. Livingstone said, "It was the first heavy stroke I have suffered, and quite takes away my strength. I wept over her, who well deserved many tears. I loved her when I married her, and the longer I lived with her I loved her the more."

How did Livingstone endure this sorrow in his life? He trusted in the God of hope to carry him through. He knew the promises of God in His Word and held on to them until his last day on earth. In fact, his African companions reportedly found him kneeling by his bed, where he had said his last earthly prayer. He stepped from time into eternity on April 30, 1873.

Who will help you when you feel as though there is no hope? The God of hope, who promises to "fill you with all joy and peace in believing, so that you will abound in hope by the power of the Holy Spirit" (Romans 15:13). Ask the Lord to quiet your heart and speak to you today about His hope for your life.

READ AND STUDY GOD'S WORD

1. Paul, called by God to take the gospel to the Gentiles, knew suffering by firsthand experience. How could he keep running the race set before him? He had learned to trust in the God of hope. Look at his words in Romans 15:13. Several translations of this most important verse are included. Underline the words and phrases most significant to you today.

"Now may the God of hope fill you with all joy and peace in believing, so that you will abound in hope by the power of the Holy Spirit."

"May the God of hope fill you with all joy and peace as you trust in him, so that you may overflow with hope by the power of the Holy Spirit" (NIV).

"May the God of your hope so fill you with all joy and peace in believing [through the experience of your faith] that by the power of the Holy Spirit you may abound *and* be overflowing (bubbling over) with hope" (AMP).

"Now the God of the hope fill you with every joy and hope in the sphere of believing, resulting in your superabounding in the sphere of the hope by the power of the Holy Spirit" (Wuest's Expanded Translation of the Greek New Testament).

2. What does it mean to hope? The Greek word translated "hope" in Romans 15:13 is *elpis* and points to the desire of some good with the expectation of obtaining it. As we have seen, you might think of HOPE as Holding On with Patient Expectation.

Peter describes your hope as a living hope (1 Peter 1:3). Kenneth Wuest defines hope this way:

> This hope is an energizing principle, a spontaneous, overflowing, buoyant thing. It is a hopefulness, a spirit of optimism, a looking ever upon the bright side of things, a looking forward to only that which is good, an expectancy of continued blessing and joy. It is the opposite of that fear of the future which grips so many hearts. This Christian optimism, this exuberant hopefulness, leaves no room for worry. This lively hope should be the normal atmosphere of every Christian heart. How may we have it? By yielding to the One whose ministry it is to produce this hopefulness in our hearts, the Holy Spirit. This Christian optimism is a heaven-born thing, something supernatural. The secret of enjoying it is in the fullness of the Holy Spirit. The secret of the fullness of the Spirit is in a moment by moment desire for that fullness, and a moment by moment trust in the Lord Jesus for the same (John 7:37-38).[6]

What will help you look to the bright side, the eternal perspective, in every situation? God's Word. God has given you an amazing treasure to grow your hope in Him. The promises of God will enable you to trust in your God and yield to His Spirit even in the midst of the most devastating of circumstances. Your broken heart, your painful experience will receive the soothing, comforting balm of God's promises, and your view will travel beyond the here and now to eternity.

Take some time now to find comfort and hope in these promises.

> "For You are my rock and my fortress; for Your name's sake You will lead and guide me" (Psalm 31:3).

> "The righteous cry, and the LORD hears and delivers them out of all their troubles. The LORD is near to the brokenhearted and saves those who are crushed in spirit" (Psalm 34:17-18).

> "God is our refuge and strength, a very present help in trouble" (Psalm 46:1).

> "Call upon Me in the day of trouble; I shall rescue you, and you will honor Me" (Psalm 50:15).

> "He heals the brokenhearted and binds up their wounds" (Psalm 147:3).

> "This I recall to my mind, therefore I have hope. The LORD's lovingkindnesses indeed never cease, for His compassions never fail. They are new every morning; great is Your faithfulness. 'The LORD is my portion,' says my soul, 'Therefore I have hope in Him'" (Lamentations 3:21-24).

> "Do not fear, for I am with you; do not anxiously look about you, for I am your God.

> "I will strengthen you, surely I will help you, surely I will uphold you with My righteous right hand" (Isaiah 41:10).

ADORE GOD IN PRAYER

Turn to the prayer pages in the back of this book and list every burden and care on your heart today. Peter says, "Give all your worries and cares to God, for he cares for you" (1 Peter 5:7 NLT).

YIELD YOURSELF TO GOD

Learn to calculate what you know about God as the great factor in every difficulty and darkness you face. Trust in the God of hope, knowing that He is at work. Draw near to Him now and meditate on these words by Octavius Winslow:

> When from the secret place of thunder He utters His voice—when, in His dealings darkness is under His feet—when he makes darkness His secret place, His pavilion round about Him dark waters and thick clouds of the skies, even then He is but making a way for His love to us, which shall appear all the more real and precious

by the very cloud-chariot in which it travels. The believer in Christ has nothing slavishly to dread, but everything filially to hope from God. So fully is he pardoned, so completely is he justified, so perfectly is he reconciled to God, the darkest dispensations in which He hides Himself shall presently unveil the brightest views of His character and love; and thus the lowering cloud that deepened in its darkness and grew larger as it approached, shall dissolve and vanish, leaving no object visible to the eye but Him whose essence and name is Love. Oh, it is because we have such shallow views of God's love that we have such defective views of God's dealings. We blindly interpret the symbols of His providence, because we so imperfectly read the engraving of His heart. Faith finds it difficult to spell the word "Love," as written in the shaded characters of its discipline; to believe that the cloud which looks so somber and threatening is the love-chariot of Him who for our ransom gave Himself unto the death, because He so loved us![7]

ENJOY HIS PRESENCE

You can know that God is always at work, even when you cannot see what He is doing. Holding on to God's promises is a great challenge, especially when you cannot comprehend His ways. God is the God of hope and intends for us to abound in hope rather than despair. What have you learned today from your quiet time that gives you hope? Articulate your thoughts in the space provided and then carry what you have learned with you throughout the day.

REST IN HIS LOVE

"And because of his glory and excellence, he has given us great and precious promises. These are the promises that enable you to share his divine nature and escape the world's corruption caused by human desires" (2 Peter 1:4 NLT).

TRUSTING IN THE FATHER OF MERCIES AND GOD OF ALL COMFORT

Blessed be the God and Father of our Lord Jesus Christ, the
Father of mercies and God of all comfort.

2 CORINTHIANS 1:3

PREPARE YOUR HEART

Where do you run in a time of trouble? Who is the one to speak calming words to you when you receive news that shakes your world? You need to draw near to the Father of mercies and the God of all comfort. He is the only one who truly knows the deepest need of your heart and can apply His healing and comforting words in your life.

Read Psalm 31:9-24 as a preparation of heart for your quiet time. Then ask the Lord to speak to you as you draw near to Him.

READ AND STUDY GOD'S WORD

1. Paul, in his second letter to the Corinthian church, shares two wonderful names of God that are especially precious for those who are in a painful and broken place, wounded by hurt, or grieved by a loss. Read 2 Corinthians 1:3-5 and write out everything you learn about God.

2. The Greek word translated "mercies" is *oiktirmo* and can also be translated "compassion" or "pity." The Greek word translated "comfort" is *paraklesis* ("encouragement.") F.B. Meyer says, "All our mercies emanate from the Father's heart, and all comfort comes from the Comforter. When next passing through great sorrow and trial, notice how near God comes and what He says." The Lord is, in fact, "near to the brokenhearted and saves those who are crushed in spirit" (Psalm 34:18). Why? Because He is the Father of mercies and the God of all comfort. His very nature drives Him to give you blessed mercies and the very comfort you need in your affliction, whatever it may be. Is your heart broken? Run to Him, for He is the Lord of broken hearts and especially

draws near to those who are crushed in spirit. Are you grieving the loss of someone dear to you? Or are you suffering the death of a dream? You can know that "The LORD's love never ends; his mercies never stop. They are new every morning" (Lamentations 3:22-23 NCV).

Reflect on the following verses and write out everything you learn about your Lord:

Psalm 23:4

Psalm 119:50

Isaiah 49:15-16

Isaiah 51:12

Isaiah 58:11

Jeremiah 31:3

Ephesians 2:4-8

Hebrews 13:5-6

3. Summarize in two or three sentences what you have learned in the Word of God today.

ADORE GOD IN PRAYER

Use the words of Annie Johnson Flint as you talk with your Lord in prayer, trusting in Him as the Father of mercies and God of all comfort:

> One day at a time, with its failures and fears,
> With its hurts and mistakes, with its weakness and tears,
> With its portion of pain and its burden of care;
> One day at a time we must meet and must bear.
>
> One day at a time to be patient and strong,
> To be calm under trial and sweet under wrong,
> Then its toiling shall pass and its sorrow shall cease;
> It shall darken and die, and the night shall bring peace.
>
> One day at a time—but the day is so long,
> And the heart is not brave and the soul is not strong.
> O Thou pitiful Christ, be Thou near all the way;
> Give courage and patience and strength for the day.
>
> Swift cometh His answer, so clear and so sweet;
> "Yea, I will be with thee, thy troubles to meet;
> I will not forget thee, nor fail thee, nor grieve;
> I will not forsake thee; I never will leave."
>
> Not yesterday's load we are called on to bear,
> Nor the morrow's uncertain and shadowy care;
> Why should we look forward or back with dismay?
> Our needs, as our mercies, are but for the day.
>
> One day at a time, and the day is His day;
> He hath numbered its hours, though they haste or delay,
> His grace is sufficient; we walk not alone;
> As the day, so the strength that He giveth His own.[8]

YIELD YOURSELF TO GOD

Reflect on these words by Hannah Whitall Smith:

> Among all the names that reveal God, this, the *God of all comfort,* seems to me one of the loveliest and the most absolutely comforting. The words *all comfort* admit of no limitations and no deductions; and one would suppose that, however full of discomforts the outward life of the followers of such a God might be, their inward religious life must necessarily be always and under all circumstances a comfortable life…Divine comfort does not come to us in any mysterious or arbitrary way. It comes as the result of a divine method. The indwelling Comforter "brings to our remembrance" comforting things concerning our Lord, and, if we believe them, we are comforted by them. A text is brought to our remembrance, perhaps, or the verse of a hymn, or some thought concerning the love of Christ and His tender care for us. If we receive the suggestion in simple faith, we cannot help being comforted.[9]

"For whatever was written in earlier times was written for our instruction, so that through perseverance and the encouragement of the Scriptures we might have hope" (Romans 15:4).

ENJOY HIS PRESENCE

What have you learned today that will help you run to the Father of mercies and God of all comfort and trust in Him?

REST IN HIS LOVE

"Can a woman forget her nursing child and have no compassion on the son of her womb? Even these may forget, but I will not forget you. Behold, I have inscribed you on the palms of My hands; Your walls are continually before Me" (Isaiah 49:15-16).

TRUSTING IN THE ALPHA AND THE OMEGA

It is done. I am the Alpha and the Omega, the beginning and the end. I will give to the one who thirsts from the spring of the water of life without cost. He who overcomes will inherit these things, and I will be his God and he will be My son.

REVELATION 21:6-7

PREPARE YOUR HEART

It is fitting in our last full day of quiet time together that we look at a name of God in the last book of the Bible. God is referred to as *the Alpha and the Omega* three times in the book of Revelation. Alpha is the first letter of the Greek alphabet, and omega is the last letter. This name reveals God's eternal existence and sovereignty. And in giving His name as the Alpha and the Omega, the beginning and the end, He is assuring you that He is the originator and completer of all things.[10] Ask God to prepare your heart and speak to you in His Word today.

READ AND STUDY GOD'S WORD

1. We began our quiet times with the name *Elohim*, the very first name of God in the Bible. Its appearance in the very first verse in Genesis almost suggests God is giving us His signature on His book, the Bible. One of the very last names of God in the Bible, *the Alpha and the Omega*, appears three times in Revelation (in 1:8; 21:6; 22:13). God says, "It is done. I am the Alpha and the Omega, the beginning and the end. I will give to the one who thirsts from the spring of the water of life without cost. He who overcomes will inherit these things, and I will be his God and he will be My son" (Revelation 21:6-7).

Gaebelein points to this name, *the Alpha and the Omega*, as a seal on all that God has said in His Word. George Eldon Ladd says that *the Alpha and the Omega* shows us that "God is the absolute beginning and the end, and therefore Lord of all that happens in human history. He is at the same time the eternal one, the transcendent one, who is unaffected by the conflicts of human history, the one who is and who was and who is to come. As the one who is to come, he will yet visit men to bring history to its divinely decreed consummation."[11] Robert Mounce, in his commentary on Revelation, says, "Alpha and Omega represent the Hebrew *Aleph Tau*, which was regarded not simply as the first and last letters of the alphabet, but as including all the letters in between. Hence, God is the sovereign Lord of all that takes place in the entire course of human history." In addition, according to Mounce, God "is not subject to the vagrancies of time because time itself is encompassed by his eternal nature."[12] Robert Bratcher explains that this name might be translated, "I am before all things, and I will continue to be after all things."[13] William Newell says that this name for God calls attention instantly away from every creature-claim—God is *all!* He is not a beginning and an end, but the only one.

Look at the following occurrences of *the Alpha and the Omega* in Revelation and write out what you learn about God:

Revelation 1:8

Revelation 22:13

2. Look at the following verses in Isaiah and write out what you learn about God:

Isaiah 41:4

Isaiah 44:6-8

3. How do you need to trust in the Alpha and the Omega today, acknowledging His sovereignty in your own life? In what ways do you need to say along with the psalmist, "The LORD will accomplish what concerns me; your lovingkindness, O LORD, is everlasting; do not forsake the works of Your hands" (Psalm 138:8)?

4. Take a few moments and look through your quiet times over the past eight weeks. What are the most important truths you have learned that help you to trust in God? Write them out in the space provided.

ADORE GOD IN PRAYER

Reflect and pray through the words of this prayer found on the flyleaf of the Bible of a missionary who died in Africa:

> Laid on Thine altar, O My Lord divine,
> Accept this gift today for Jesus' sake.
> I have worn no jewels to adorn Thy shrine,
> Nor any world-famed sacrifice to make;
> But here I bring within my trembling hand
> This will of mine that seemeth small,
> And Thou alone, O Lord, canst understand
> How when I yield Thee this I yield my all.
>
> Hidden therein Thy searching gaze can see
> Struggles of passion, visions of delight;
> All that I have, or am, or fain would be;
> Deep loves, fond hopes, and longings infinite.
> It hath been wet with tears and dimmed with sighs,
> Clenched in my grasp till beauty hath it none!
> Now from Thy footstool, where it vanquished lies,
> The prayer ascendeth—may Thy will be done!
>
> Take I, O Father, ere my courage fail,
> And merge it so in Thine own will that e'en,
> If in some desperate hour my cries prevail
> And Thou give back my gift, it may have been

So changed, so purified, so fair have grown,
So one with Thee, so filled with peace divine,
I may not know or feel it as mine own;
But, gaining back my will, may find it Thine.[14]

YIELD YOURSELF TO GOD

Think about the words of this poem, the favorite of Charles Cowman, husband of the author of *Streams in the Desert:*

My heart is there! Where on eternal hills, my loved one dwells
Among the lilies and asphodels;
Clad in the brightness of the Great White Throne,
Glad in the smile of Him who sits thereon,
The glory gilding all His wealth of hair
And making His immortal face more fair—
There is my treasure and my heart is there.

My heart is there! With Him who made all earthly life so sweet,
So fit to live, and yet to die so meet;
So mild, so grand, so gentle and so brave,
So ready to forgive, so strong to save.
His fair, pure Spirit makes the Heavens more fair,
And thither rises all my longing prayer—
There is my treasure and my heart is there.[15]

ENJOY HIS PRESENCE

What a treasure you have in the names, character, and attributes of God! May your heart always be abiding with your dear Lord. You have journeyed through some of the most exciting names of God, exploring His character and gazing at some of His choice attributes. But don't stop now. Many more beauties in the character of God are yet to be discovered as you traverse the landscape of God's Word.

Never allow any area of your Bible to remain buried and unknown to you. Instead, resolve to continue the journey every day and live in every corner of God's Word. Set aside a time, choose a quiet place, and sit with the Lord each day with an open Bible and an open heart. I encourage you to engage in the 30-day companion journey of *Trusting in the Names of God* (Harvest House Publishers) and explore the resources available through Quiet Time Ministries. Dear friend, what a joy to journey together with you. Always remember, this is not the end, but only a very exciting beginning of the great adventure. And so, God bless you as you continue on in this great adventure of knowing Him.

In the introduction, you wrote a letter to the Lord. Take some time now to read your letter again. How has God answered your prayer and met you in His Word? Close by writing a new letter, a prayer of thanksgiving to your Lord.

I saw an aged Pilgrim,
Whose toilsome march was o'er,
With slow and painful footstep
Approaching Jordan's shore:
He first his dusty vestment
And sandals cast aside,
Then, with an air of transport,
Enter'd the swelling tide.

I thought to see him shudder,
As cold the waters rose,
And fear'd lest o'er him, surging,
The murky stream should close;
But calmly and unshrinking,
The billowy path he trod,
And cheer'd with Jesus' presence,
Pass'd o'er the raging flood.

On yonder shore to greet him,
I saw a shining throng;
Some just begun their praising,
Some had been praising long;
With joy they bade him welcome,
And struck their harps again,
While through the heavenly arches
Peal'd the triumphal strain.

Now in a robe of glory,
And with a starry crown,
I see the weary Pilgrim
With Kings and Priests sit down;
With Prophets, Patriarchs, Martyrs,
And Saints, a countless throng,
He chants his great deliverance,
In never-ceasing song.[16]

OCTAVIUS WINSLOW

REST IN HIS LOVE

"And I heard a loud voice from the throne, saying, 'Behold, the tabernacle of God is among men, and He will dwell among them, and they shall be His people, and God Himself will be among them, and He will wipe away every tear from their eyes; and there will no longer be any death; there will no longer be any mourning, or crying or pain; the first things have passed away'" (Revelation 21:3-4).

DEVOTIONAL READING
BY MRS. CHARLES E. COWMAN

You cannot detain the eagle in the forest. You may gather around him a chorus of the choicest birds; you may give him a perch on the goodliest pine; you may charge winged messengers to bring him choicest dainties; but he will spurn them all. Spreading his lofty wings, and with his eye on the Alpine cliff, he will soar away to his own ancestral halls amid the munition of rocks and the wild music of tempest and waterfall. The soul of man, in its eagle soarings, will rest with nothing short of the Rock of Ages. Its ancestral halls are the halls of Heaven. Its munitions of rocks are the attributes of God. The sweep of its majestic flight is Eternity! "Lord, Thou hast been our dwelling place in all generations."

> "My Home is God Himself"; Christ brought me there.
> I laid me down within His mighty arms;
> He took me up, and safe from all alarms
> He bore me "where no foot but His hath trod,"
> Within the holiest at Home with God,
> And bade me dwell in Him, rejoicing there.
> O Holy Place! O Home divinely fair!
> And we, God's little ones, abiding there.

> "My Home is God Himself": it was not so!
> A long, long road I traveled night and day,
> And sought to find within myself some way,
> Aught I could do, or feel to bring me near;
> Self effort failed, and I was filled with fear,
> And then I found Christ was the only way,
> That I must come to Him and in Him stay,
> And God had told me so.

And now "my Home is God," and sheltered there,
God meets the trials of my earthly life,
God compasses me round from storm and strife,
God takes the burden of my daily care,
O Wondrous Place! O Home divinely fair!
And I, God's little one, safe hidden there.
Lord, as I dwell in Thee and Thou in me,
So make me dead to everything but Thee;
That as I rest within my Home most fair,
My soul may evermore and only see
My God is everything and everywhere;
My Home is God.[17]

Take some time now to write about all that you have learned this week and throughout this quiet time experience. What has been most significant to you? Close by writing a prayer to the Lord.

ᚬᚣ Discussion Questions ᚣᚬ

Introduction

Begin your class with prayer and then welcome everyone to this new book of quiet times. Have the people in your group share their names and what brought them to the study. Make sure each person in your group has a book. Also, gather contact information for all participants in your group including name, address, phone number, and e-mail. That way you can keep in touch and encourage those in your group.

Familiarize your group with the layout of the book. Each week consists of five days of quiet times, as well as a devotional reading and response for days 6 and 7. Each day follows the PRAYER quiet time plan:

> Prepare Your Heart
>
> Read and Study God's Word
>
> Adore God in Prayer
>
> Yield Yourself to God
>
> Enjoy His Presence
>
> Rest in His Love

Journal and prayer pages are included in the back of the book. Note that the quiet times offer devotional reading, Bible study, prayer, and practical application.

You can determine how to organize your group sessions, but here's one idea: Discuss the week of quiet times together in the first hour, break for ten minutes, and then watch the message on the companion DVD. There are nine messages for this quiet time experience—one for the introduction and one for each week. You might also share with your group a summary of how to prepare for their quiet time by setting aside a time each day and a place. Consider sharing how time alone with the Lord has made a difference in your own life. Let your class know about the Quiet Time Ministries websites: www.quiettime.org and www.myquiettime.com.

Another option is to divide each week (completing the study in 16 weeks) by discussing days 1–3 one week and days 4–7 another week. This allows your group to journey through each quiet time at a slower pace.

Pray for one another by offering a way to record and exchange prayer requests. Some groups like to pass around a basket with cards that people can use to record prayer requests. Then, people take a request out of the basket and pray for someone during the week. Others like to use three by five cards and then exchange cards on a weekly basis.

Close this introductory class with prayer, take a short break, and show the companion DVD message.

Week One: A Heart for the Lord

DAY 1: The One Thing

Welcome everyone to this quiet time experience. In this first week you had the opportunity to consider the meaning and importance of having a heart for the Lord.

1. What encouraged you most in the introduction? Why is spending time to know God so important? What phrase meant the most to you from Tozer's quote on page 13?

2. In day 1, what did David's example teach you about having a heart for the Lord? What did David want more than anything?

3. What does it mean to be a "one thing" person?

DAY 2: Seeking the Lord

1. In day 2 you had the opportunity to think about seeking the Lord. What does it mean to seek the Lord?

2. What did you learn about seeking the Lord? According to the verses you looked at in the Bible, what is the value of seeking the Lord?

3. What was your favorite quote from day 2?

4. Having thought about seeking of the Lord yourself, would you like to share with your group anything from the response section in "Enjoy His Presence"?

DAY 3: Living with the Lord

1. In day 3 you looked at David's statement about dwelling in the house of the Lord all the days of his life. What did David really want in life?

2. What did you learn about God from the different translations of Deuteronomy 33:27 and Psalm 37:23?

3. What decisions and resolves would you need to make to live with the Lord and

walk with Him day by day? How did thinking about this help you to draw near to God and know Him better?

DAY 4: Looking at His Beauty

1. How do God's names help you know and trust God more?

2. What is significant about a name of God?

3. What are the benefits of knowing the names of God?

4. Over the past few years, what has been the most important truth you have learned about God? How has what you've learned changed the way you live your life?

DAY 5: Learning About His Ways

1. What did the examples of David and Moses teach you about having a heart for the Lord?

2. How does the Bible help you know God better?

DAYS 6 AND 7: Devotional Reading by F.B. Meyer

1. What was your favorite verse, insight, or quote from your quiet times this week?

2. What did you learn from the excerpt by F.B. Meyer on page 35?

3. What is the most important truth you learned this week about having a heart for the Lord? How can you apply it in your own life?

Week Two: Trusting in the Lord

DAY 1: The Foundation of Trust

Begin today by summarizing what you learned in week 1 about having a heart for the Lord. This week we looked at what it means to trust in the Lord.

1. What phrase from Hannah Whitall Smith's quote at the beginning of week 2 meant the most to you?

2. What was your favorite verse from Psalm 9?

3. What does *trusting the Lord* mean?

4. Why does knowing God's names help you trust in Him?

5. What was your favorite quote from the Puritan devotional prayer or the excerpt by Charles Spurgeon?

DAY 2: The Prayer of Trust

1. What was your favorite truth from Psalm 25?

2. How does crying out to the Lord and declaring who God is, what He does, and what He says help you to trust God?

3. How did David trust the Lord in the midst of the threat from his son Absalom?

4. What can you learn from David and his prayers that will help you the next time you face a difficulty in your own life?

DAY 3: The Test of Trust

1. How do trials test your trust in God?

2. What did you learn from Psalm 22 about trusting God in trials?

3. How has your trust in God been tested?

4. What have you learned that will help you trust God more in your own trials?

DAY 4: The Result of Trust

1. What happens when you trust in God? How does God respond?

2. What did you learn about the Lord's help from the verses included in your quiet time today?

3. What did you learn today that will help you trust the Lord?

DAY 5: The Declaration of Trust

1. Day 5 began with a question: "Could you be called God's cheerleader or the world's complainer?" How did you answer that question in your own mind?

2. What was your favorite phrase from the hymn "O for a Thousand Tongues to Sing"?

3. What was your favorite insight from Psalm 20?

DAYS 6 AND 7: Devotional Reading by Alan Redpath

1. What was your favorite verse, insight, or quote from your quiet times this week?

2. What did you learn from the excerpt by Alan Redpath on page 61?

3. What is the most important truth you learned about trusting God this week? How can you apply it in your own life, and how will it help you trust God more?

Week Three: Behold His Beauty in Creation

DAY 1: Behold Your God

1. Open your discussion with prayer. Briefly review last week's discussion and David's example of trusting God. Also review the importance of the names of God and how they reveal the character and attributes of God.

2. What phrase meant the most to you from Stephen Charnock's quote on page 67?

3. This week you had the opportunity to begin thinking about the nature of God: who He is, what He does, and what He says. What did you learn about how God has revealed Himself to us?

4. The first name of God you looked at is *Elohim*. What did you learn about *Elohim?*

DAY 2: The Day God Painted the Sky

1. What was most profound to you in day 2 as you considered God and all that He has created?

2. Would you like to share with your group anything from your prayer in "Enjoy His Presence"?

DAY 3: The Day God Sculpted a Man

1. How does knowing that God created you influence the way you view yourself? How does this truth influence the way you view others?

2. What was your most important insight from Psalm 139?

3. What did you learn about the wisdom of God?

4. What is God showing you about Himself that helps you trust in Him?

DAY 4: The Day God Answered Job

1. How does suffering challenge our ability to trust in God?

2. What did you learn from Job and from God's revelation of Himself to Job?

3. What did you learn in day 4 that will help you trust God in a time of trouble?

DAY 5: Trusting in Elohim

1. How has God become more personal to you as you have studied His name *Elohim?*

2. What did you learn about Elohim in day 5?

3. What is your favorite truth about Elohim from this week of quiet times?

DAYS 6 AND 7: Devotional Reading by Matthew Henry

1. In days 6 and 7 you had the opportunity to read from Matthew Henry. What was your favorite truth from his writing?

2. You closed your week by writing a prayer to the Lord. Would you be willing to read all or part of your prayer?

3. Close your time by praying F.B. Meyer's prayer in "Adore God in Prayer" on page 78.

Week Four: Behold His Beauty with the Friend of God

DAY 1: The Day God Made a Friend

1. Open your discussion with prayer. Briefly review your discussion last week about the name *Elohim*. You saw that God reveals Himself progressively over time and that you can discover His names in His Word. This week we had the opportunity to look at the life of Abraham and how God revealed Himself to him. What is Abraham's greatest claim to fame?

2. What do you think made Abraham such a friend of God?

3. When God first revealed Himself to Abraham, what did He ask of Abraham, and what did He promise?

4. What was your favorite quote in today's reading in your quiet time?

DAY 2: Calling on the Name of the Lord

1. What did you learn from Abraham about prayer and calling on the name of the Lord?

2. What does *calling on the name of the Lord* mean?

3. In the past week, how did you need to call on the name of the Lord?

DAY 3: El Shaddai—A Great God for a Great Promise

1. In day 3 you learned that God made a huge promise to Abraham. Why was His promise seemingly impossible?

2. God revealed Himself as *El Shaddai* ("God Almighty") to Abraham. What did you learn about the name *El Shaddai*, and why was God's revelation of this name so relevant to Abraham at this time in his life?

3. How did God fulfill His promise to Abraham?

4. How do you need El Shaddai in your own life? How does knowing that God is the all-sufficient one encourage you?

DAY 4: El Olam—An Eternal God for an Eternal Friend

1. In day 4 you learned a new name for God—*El Olam.* What did you learn about the name *El Olam?*

2. How does knowing El Olam encourage a person in life?

3. What did you learn about the eternal nature of God from the verses listed on page 102?

4. What did you learn about your friendship with Jesus? What does having the opportunity for this great friendship mean to you?

5. What was your favorite quote in day 4?

DAY 5: The Triumph of a Great Trust

1. In day 5 you saw that Abraham was tested. How was he tested?

2. How did the test reveal Abraham's character, and what did you learn about Abraham?

3. What did you learn about Yahweh Jireh? How do you need Yahweh Jireh today?

4. What impresses you most about the example of Abraham?

5. What was your favorite quote from today's quiet time?

DAYS 6 AND 7: Devotional Reading by A.W. Tozer

1. In days 6 and 7 you had the opportunity to read from A.W. Tozer. What was your favorite truth from his writing?

2. What was the most important truth you learned this week?

3. Did you have a favorite quote? A favorite verse?

4. Close in prayer.

Week Five: Behold His Beauty with the People Who Lived with God

DAY 1: The Divine Interruption of God

1. Open your discussion with prayer. Briefly review last week's discussion about Abraham, the friend of God. We saw that God revealed Himself to Abraham as *El Shaddai, El Olam,* and *Yahweh Jireh.* Then we learned about how we too are granted the privilege of intimate friendship with God.

   This week, we have journeyed with Moses as he was granted the privilege of an intimate relationship with God. In day 1, you saw what was called "the divine interruption of God." How did God divinely interrupt Moses' life?

2. Moses was called a man of God. What made Moses a man of God?

3. How did Moses respond to God when He called out Moses' name?

4. What is your favorite insight from A.W. Tozer's excerpt on page 117?

5. How has God divinely interrupted your life, and how did you respond to Him? What can you learn from Moses' example and his response to God?

DAY 2: Trusting in the God Who Sees

1. In day 2 you learned that God made a very important statement: "I have surely seen the affliction of My people who are in Egypt" (Exodus 3:7). You learned that God is *El Roi* ("the God who sees"). How was El Roi an encouragement to Hagar?

2. What is so encouraging about the name *El Roi?*

3. How will trusting in El Roi make a difference in a person's life?

DAY 3: Trusting in the Great I AM

1. In day 3 you learned about the name *Yahweh.* How did God reveal His name *Yahweh* to Moses?

2. What does the name *Yahweh* mean, and why is it such an important name of God?

3. What were some of your favorite insights about Yahweh from your time in God's Word?

4. What was your favorite quote from day 3?

DAY 4: Daring to Draw Near

1. Moses was the most humble man on the face of the earth, and yet he dared to draw near to God. What did you learn from the relationship between God and Moses?

2. What did Moses learn about God after his request to know God more?

3. How can you experience the glory of God?

4. How can Moses' example and the names of God he learned help you in your own trust of God?

DAY 5: Trusting in the Living God

1. In day 5 you had the opportunity to learn from Joshua and his relationship with God. What name of God was revealed to Joshua?

2. What did you learn about El Hay—the Living God?

3. Why does idolatry offend the living God?

4. What idols must we guard against in the world today?

5. You were asked to write a prayer of trust at the end of your quiet time. Would you be willing to share your prayer with your group?

DAYS 6 AND 7: Devotional Reading by F.B. Meyer

1. What was your favorite verse, insight, or quote from your quiet times this week?

2. What did you learn from the excerpt by F.B. Meyer on page 135?

3. What is the most important truth you learned about trusting God this week? How can you apply it in your own life, and how will it help you trust God more?

4. Close by reading together "The Pledge of Trust" on pages 132–133.

Week Six: Behold His Beauty with the Prophets, Who Spoke for God

DAY 1: Trusting in Your Redeemer

1. Open your discussion with prayer. Briefly review last week's discussion about God's revelation to Moses as Yahweh. Summarize what you learned about *Yahweh,* this most important name of God. Describe Moses' relationship with Yahweh. What does the name *El Roi* ("the God who sees") tell you about God?

    This week we have spent time looking at how God revealed Himself to the prophets Isaiah, Jeremiah, Ezekiel, Daniel, and Zechariah. Describe God's call of Isaiah to his prophetic ministry. What did Isaiah see? What did you learn about God in this vision given to Isaiah?

2. In day 1 you saw that Isaiah called God a Redeemer. What does *Redeemer* mean?

3. What did you learn about the Lord as your Redeemer?

4. What is a kinsman-redeemer, and how was Boaz a good example of a kinsman-redeemer?

5. How is Jesus your Redeemer? How did He accomplish your redemption?

6. What is the most important truth you learned from day 1? How does trust in Jesus as your Redeemer make a difference in your life?

DAY 2: Trusting in Yahweh Tsidkenu, the Lord Your Righteousness

1. In day 2 you learned about God from the prophet Jeremiah. Describe God's call of Jeremiah.

2. What does the name *Yahweh Tsidkenu* mean?

3. What did you learn about Jesus as your righteousness? How does knowing and trusting in Jesus as your righteousness make a difference in your life?

DAY 3: Trusting in Yahweh Shammah, the Lord Is There

1. What impressed you about the story of Amanda Smith?

2. What must it have been like for Ezekiel to receive the vision described in Ezekiel 1?

3. What was God asking of Ezekiel in Ezekiel 2?

4. One of the names of God revealed to Ezekiel was *Yahweh Shammah.* What did you learn about this name of God?

5. How does knowing and trusting in Yahweh Shammah encourage you today?

DAY 4: Trusting in El Elyon, God Most High

1. One of the prophets who trusted in God was Daniel. One of the most repeated names of God in Daniel is *El Elyon.* What does the name *El Elyon* mean?

2. How are we to respond to El Elyon?

3. What did you learn from God's work in Joseph's life?

4. What did you learn about God's sovereignty? How does knowing God is sovereign make a difference in your own life?

5. What does trusting in El Elyon involve? How can we trust in Him?

DAY 5: Trusting in Yahweh Sabaoth, the Lord of Hosts

1. In day 5 you learned about the name *Yahweh Sabaoth.* Describe Yahweh Sabaoth and what trusting in Him means.

2. How did Jesus deliver His people?

3. How does David exemplify trusting in Yahweh Sabaoth?

4. What giants have you faced or are you facing? How does trusting in Yahweh Sabaoth encourage you today?

DAYS 6 AND 7: Devotional Reading by J.I. Packer

1. What was your favorite verse, insight, or quote from your quiet times this week?

2. What did you learn from the excerpt by J.I. Packer on page 163?

3. What is the most important truth you learned about trusting God this week? How can you apply it in your own life, and how will what you have learned help you trust God more?

4. Close in prayer.

Week Seven: Behold His Beauty with Jesus, the Son of God

DAY 1: He Has Explained Him

1. Open your discussion with prayer.

   Share briefly about all that we have been looking at in the names of God. We began by looking at what it means to have a heart for the Lord and to trust in the names of God, including *Elohim*. We considered growing in our friendship with God as we trust in Him as *El Shaddai, El Olam, El Roi,* and *Yahweh Jireh.* We discussed living with Yahweh, who is the living God, and drawing near to God through names we learned from the prophets. He is the Redeemer, the Lord our righteousness, the Lord who is there, God Most High, and the Lord of hosts.

   Now, in week 7, we had the opportunity to know God more intimately through Jesus. Begin by reading the quote by Tozer on page 165.

   What did you learn about Jesus in day 1?

2. Why does knowing Christ help us understand who God is, what God does, and what God says?

3. What is the most important truth you learned about Christ?

DAY 2: The Eternal I AM

1. You have already learned about Yahweh through your study in the life of Moses. Now you learned a new truth about Yahweh. Jesus is the exact representation and explanation of God (John 1:18; Hebrews 1:3). How did Jesus explain Yahweh?

2. What did you learn from the I AM statements of Jesus? Who is Jesus?

3. What was your favorite part of the prayer on pages 173–174?

4. In what way do you need to trust in Jesus as Yahweh, who is everything you need for every circumstance of life?

DAY 3: The Beauty of the Lord

1. In day 3 you gained a view into the heart of God through Jesus. What did you learn about the beauty of your Lord?

2. How does what you have learned help you trust your Lord more?

3. What was your favorite quote from your quiet time in day 3?

DAY 4: Intimate Communion

1. Jesus enjoyed intimate communion with the Father. And you can also enjoy this beautiful communion with your Lord. What do you learn from the example of Jesus that will encourage you in your own time alone with the Lord?

2. When Jesus taught the disciples to pray, He said "Hallowed be Your name." What did He mean when He prayed those words?

3. What did you learn about the holiness of God?

4. What was your favorite part of Jesus' conversation with the Father in John 17?

5. How does the example of Jesus' quiet time encourage you in your quiet time?

DAY 5: Abba! Father!

1. In day 5 you learned a new name for God: *Abba, Father.* What did you learn about this name of God?

2. How did the illustration by Jeanette Clift George (see page 187) help you understand your relationship with your heavenly Father?

3. Why was it especially significant that Jesus used this name of God when He was in the garden of Gethsemane? How does His use of this name help you understand how to trust in Abba, Father?

4. Why are we now given the privilege to address God as *Abba Father?*

5. How does knowing God is your Father encourage you?

DAYS 6 AND 7: Devotional Reading by Charles Spurgeon

1. What was your favorite verse, insight, or quote from your quiet times this week?

2. What did you learn from the excerpt by Charles Spurgeon on pages 191?

3. What is the most important truth you learned about trusting God this week? How can you apply it in your own life, and how will it help you trust God more?

Week Eight: Behold His Beauty with the Disciples Who Walked with God

DAY 1: When You See His Glory

1. Open your discussion with prayer.

   Begin by expressing how much you've enjoyed leading the group and sharing together during this quiet time experience. Encourage your class or group to not miss out on the companion 30-day journey of *Trusting in the Names of God*.

   What has been your favorite part of this eight-week quiet time experience?

2. This week you had the opportunity to see the Lord through the eyes of the disciples. One of their great experiences occurred when Jesus took Peter, James, and John up on a high mountain. Describe what happened from Matthew 17:1-8.

3. What did you learn about the glory of God?

4. How do we have the opportunity to experience the glory of God now?

DAY 2: When You Experience His Power

1. In day 2 you learned about the power of God. Describe the life of Francis Asbury and how the power of God made a difference in his life (see page 199).

2. Why is Paul such a great example of what God's power can do in a life?

3. What did you learn about God's power?

4. How do you need His power today?

DAY 3: Trusting in the God of Hope

1. Read Romans 15:13. What name for God does Paul share in this verse?

2. What does it mean to hope in God?

3. Describe how God's hope is different from the world's hope.

4. Share a promise from God's Word that gives you hope today.

5. What was your favorite quote from day 3?

6. How do you need to trust in the God of hope? How has the God of hope been an encouragement to you?

DAY 4: Trusting in the Father of Mercies and God of All Comfort

1. Read 2 Corinthians 1:3-5. What names of God do these verses reveal?

2. What does the word *mercies* mean?

3. What does the word *comfort* mean?

4. Why are these two names of God such an encouragement?

5. What was the most important truth about God that you learned from the verses listed in day 4?

6. What was your favorite quote from day 4?

DAY 5: Trusting in the Alpha and the Omega

1. What did you learn about the Alpha and the Omega in day 5? What does that name of God mean?

2. How will trusting in the Alpha and the Omega make a difference in a person's life?

3. You had an opportunity to leaf through these eight weeks of quiet times to look at all you have learned. What have we learned about trusting in God in this study?

4. What is the most important truth you have learned about God in this book of quiet times? What will you take with you?

5. How did God answer the prayer you wrote in your letter to Him at the beginning of the study?

DAYS 6 AND 7: Devotional Reading by Mrs. Charles E. Cowman

1. What was your favorite verse, insight, or quote from your quiet times this week and from the entire book of quiet times?

2. What encouraged you from the excerpt from *Streams in the Desert* on pages 219–220?

3. How has this study increased your trust in your God? How has it encouraged your intimacy with your Lord?

4. Close in prayer.

❧ NOTES ❧

INTRODUCTION

1. Amy Carmichael, *Gold Cord* (Fort Washington: Christian Literature Crusade), p. 195.

WEEK 1

Epigraph. A.W. Tozer, *The Pursuit of God* (Camp Hill: Christian Publications, 1993), p. 7.

1. Henry Law, *Daily Prayer and Praise*, vol. 1 (Carlisle: Banner of Truth Trust, 2000), pp. 136-37.

2. F.B. Meyer, *Devotional Commentary* (Wheaton: Tyndale House, 1989), p. 236.

3. F.B. Meyer, *Daily Prayers* (Wheaton: Harold Shaw, 1995), p. 58.

4. Charles Spurgeon, *The Treasury of David*, vol. 1 (McLean: MacDonald, n.d.), pp. 2-3.

5. Octavius Winslow, *Our God*, published in 1870. Available online at www.gracegems.org/winslow/our%20god.htm.

6. A.W. Tozer, *The Pursuit of God* (Camp Hill: Christian Publications, 1993), pp. 85-86, 89-90.

7. Quoted in W.Y. Fullerton, *F.B. Meyer: A Biography* (London: Marshall, Morgan and Scott), pp. 59-60.

8. Winslow, *Our God.*

9. F.B. Meyer, *David: Shepherd, Psalmist, King* (New York: Revell, 1895), n.p.

WEEK 2

Epigraph. Hannah Whitall Smith, *The Christian's Secret of a Happy Life* (New York: Revell, 1941), pp. 76-77.

1. Quoted in Warren W. Wiersbe, *Living with the Giants* (Grand Rapids: Baker Book House, 1993), p. 176.

2. Herbert Lockyer, *Psalms: A Devotional Commentary* (Grand Rapids: Kregel, 1993), pp. 37-38.

3. Arthur Bennett, ed., "God Enjoyed," *The Valley of Vision* (Carlisle: Banner of Truth Trust, 2001), p. 11.

4. Charles Spurgeon, *Morning and Evening* (Peabody: Hendrickson, 2005), March 7 p.m.

5. Lockyer, *Psalms,* p. 94.

6. Henry Law, *Daily Prayer and Praise,* vol. 1 (Carlisle: Banner of Truth Trust, 2000), p. 123.

7. Quoted in Mrs. Charles Cowman, *Springs in the Valley* (Los Angeles: Oriental Missionary Society, 1939), p. 201.

8. F.B. Meyer, *Daily Prayers* (Wheaton: Harold Shaw, 1995), p. 11.

9. F.B. Meyer, *Devotional Commentary* (Wheaton: Tyndale House, 1989), p. 235.

10. Spurgeon, *Morning and Evening,* August 31 a.m.

11. Amy Carmichael, *Mountain Breezes* (Fort Washington: Christian Literature Crusade, 1999), p. 167.

12. Alan Redpath, *The Making of a Man of God* (Old Tappan: Revell, 1962), p. 174.

WEEK 3

Epigraph. Stephen Charnock, *Discourses upon the Existence and Attributes of God,* vol. 1 (Grand Rapids: Baker Book House, 1979), p. 43.

1. R. Laird Harris, Gleason L. Archer Jr., and Bruce K. Waltke, *Theological Wordbook of the Old Testament,* vol. 1 (Chicago: Moody Press, 1999), pp. 39-40.

2. F.B. Meyer, *Daily Prayers* (Wheaton: Harold Shaw, 1995), p. 58.

3. Charnock, *The Existence and Attributes of God,* vol. 1, pp. 43-44.

4. Henry Law, *Daily Prayer and Praise,* vol. 1 (Carlisle: Banner of Truth Trust, 2000), pp. 91-92.

5. Gypsy Smith, *As Jesus Passed By* (Old Tappan: Revell, 1905), p. 16.

6. Larry Richards, *The 365 Day Devotional Commentary* (Wheaton: Victor Books, 1990), p. 5.

7. Meyer, *Daily Prayers,* p. 60.

8. Charles Spurgeon and Roy H. Clarke, *Beside Still Waters* (Nashville: Thomas Nelson, 2000), p. 73.

9. Samuel Rutherford, *The Letters of Samuel Rutherford* (Carlisle: Banner of Truth Trust, 1984), p. 333.

10. A.W. Tozer, *The Knowledge of the Holy* (New York: HarperCollins, 1992), pp. 43-44.

11. Matthew Henry, *Matthew Henry's Commentary on the Whole Bible* (Peabody: Hendrickson, 1996). From the commentary on Genesis 1:1.

WEEK 4

Epigraph. Dwight Hervey Small, *No Rival Love* (Fort Washington: Christian Literature Crusade, 1984), p. 104.

1. Small, *No Rival Love,* pp. 87-89.

2. F.B. Meyer, *Devotional Commentary* (Wheaton: Tyndale House, 1989), p. 18.

3. Meyer, *Devotional Commentary,* p. 559.

4. A.W. Tozer, *Men Who Met God* (Camp Hill: Christian Publications, 1986), pp. 9-11.

5. Stephen Charnock, *Discourses upon the Existence and Attributes of God* (Grand Rapids: Baker Book House, 1979), pp. 281-99.

6. James Montgomery Boice, *Genesis: An Expositional Commentary* (Grand Rapids: Baker Books, 1998), p. 676.

7. Small, *No Rival Love,* p. 86.

8. F.B. Meyer, *Daily Prayers* (Wheaton: Harold Shaw, 1995), p. 66.

9. Small, *No Rival Love,* pp. 99-103.

10. Tozer, *Men Who Met God,* pp. 13-14.

WEEK 5

Epigraph. F..B. Meyer (1847–1929), *Exodus.* Accessed online.

1. A.W. Tozer, *Men Who Met God* (Camp Hill: Christian Publications, 1986), p. 72.

2. George Beverly Shea, *How Sweet the Sound* (Wheaton: Tyndale House, 2004), p. 33.

3. Charles Spurgeon, *Behold the Throne of Grace* (London: Marshall, Morgan & Scott), p. 15.

4. John Henry Jowett, *Great Pulpit Masters,* vol. 5 (New York: Revell, 1950), p. 99.

5. Gypsy Smith, *As Jesus Passed By* (Old Tappan: Revell, 1905), p. 12.

6. Herbert Lockyer, *All the Divine Names and Titles in the Bible* (Grand Rapids: Zondervan, 1975), p. 17.

7. Amy Carmichael, *Mountain Breezes* (Fort Washington: Christian Literature Crusade, 1999), p. 224.

8. Hannah Whitall Smith, *The God of All Comfort* (Chicago: Moody Press, 1956), pp. 246, 253.

9. Kenneth L. Barker, ed., *The TNIV Study Bible* (Grand Rapids: Zondervan, 2006), p. 140.

10. F.B. Meyer (1847–1929), *Moses, the Servant of God.* Accessed online.

11. Robert G. Bratcher and Barclay Moon Newman, *A Translator's Handbook on the Book of Joshua* (New York: United Bible Societies, 1983), p. 42.

12. Bryan Jeffery Leech, "The Pledge of Trust." © 1976. All rights reserved. Used by permission.

13. Quoted in Mrs. Charles Cowman, *Streams in the Desert* (Los Angeles: Oriental Missionary Society, 1925), pp. 19-20.

14. Meyer, *Moses, the Servant of God.*

WEEK 6

Epigraph. J.I. Packer, *Knowing God* (Downers Grove: InterVarsity Press, 1973), p. 30.

1. Walter Kaiser, *Back Toward the Future* (Grand Rapids: Baker Book House, 1989), pp. 21-27.

2. R. Laird Harris, Gleason L. Archer Jr., and Bruce K. Waltke, *Theological Wordbook of the Old Testament,* vol. 1 (Chicago: Moody Press, 1999), p. 144.

3. David Martyn Lloyd-Jones, *God's Ultimate Purpose* (Carlisle: Banner of Truth Trust, 1978), p. 152.

4. William Newell, *Romans Verse by Verse* (Chicago: Moody Press, 1977), pp. 97-98.

5. J. Vernon McGee, *Thru the Bible Commentary,* vol. 45, *2 Corinthians* (Nashville: Thomas Nelson, 1991), p. 74.

6. Andrew A. Bonar and Robert M. McCheyne, *Memoir and Remains of R.M. McCheyne* (Chicago: Moody Press, 1996), p. 443.

7. Lamar Eugene Cooper, *The New American Commentary,* vol. 17, *Ezekiel* (Nashville: Broadman & Holman, 2001), p. 425.

8. F.B. Meyer, *Daily Prayers* (Wheaton: Harold Shaw, 1995), p. 83.

9. Herbert Lockyer, *All the Divine Names and Titles in the Bible* (Grand Rapids: Zondervan, 1975), pp. 60-64.

10. A.C. Gaebelein, *The Prophet Daniel* (New York: E.E. Fitch, 1911), p. 9.

11. H.L. Ellison, *The Old Testament Prophets* (Grand Rapids: Zondervan, 1974), p. 145.

12. Meyer, *Daily Prayers,* p. 60.

13. Alan Redpath, *The Making of a Man of God* (Old Tappan: Revell, 1962), pp. 27-28.

14. J.I. Packer, *Knowing God* (Downers Grove: InterVarsity Press, 1973), p. 29.

WEEK 7

Epigraph. A.W. Tozer, *Men Who Met God* (Camp Hill: Christian Publications, 1986), p. 120.

1. F.B. Meyer, *Daily Prayers* (Wheaton: Harold Shaw, 1995), p. 5.

2. Alexander Balmain Bruce, *The Training of the Twelve* (Oak Harbor: Logos Research Systems, 1995), p. 400.

3. Peter Bayne, *The Testimony of Christ to Christianity* (Boston: Gould and Lincoln, 1862), pp. 197-200.

4. Quoted in Arthur Bennett, ed., *The Valley of Vision* (Carlisle: Banner of Truth Trust, 2001), p. 104.

5. James Montgomery Boice, *The Gospel of John* (Grand Rapids: Baker Books, 2005), pp. 675-76.

6. Brennan Manning, *Lion and Lamb* (Grand Rapids: Chosen Books, 1986), p. 34.

7. Alistair McGrath, *Understanding Jesus* (Grand Rapids: Zondervan, 1987), p. 141.

8. A.W. Tozer, *Christ the Eternal Son* (Camp Hill: Christian Publications, 1982), p. 29.

9. Paraphrased in David and Julian Hazard, *I Promise You a Crown* (Minneapolis: Bethany House, 1995), p. 50.

10. Quoted in Mrs. Charles Cowman, *Streams in the Desert* (Los Angeles: Oriental Missionary Society, 1925), p. 361.

11. A.W. Tozer, *The Divine Conquest* (Camp Hill, Christian Publications, 1950), p. 22.

12. Tozer, *Men Who Met God,* pp. 102-3.

13. Adapted from Claire Cloninger, *Dear Abba* (Dallas: Word, 1997) p. 8-10.

14. Bruce, *The Training of the Twelve*, p. 403.

15. Charles Spurgeon, *Morning and Evening* (Peabody: Hendrickson, 2006), January 26 a.m.

16. Spurgeon, *Morning and Evening*, October 14 a.m.

WEEK 8

Epigraph. Octavius Winslow, *Daily Walking with God.* From the devotion for January 2. Available online at www.gracegems.org/winslow/morning%20thoughts.htm.

1. Alexander Balmain Bruce, *The Training of the Twelve* (Oak Harbor: Logos Research Systems, 1995), p. 41.

2. F.B. Meyer, *Daily Prayers* (Wheaton: Harold Shaw, 1995), p. 57.

3. Charles Spurgeon, *Morning and Evening* (Peabody: Hendrickson, 2006), August 26 p.m.

4. See Wesley L. Duewel, *Heroes of the Holy Life* (Grand Rapids: Zondervan, 2002), p. 20.

5. John Henry Jowett, *The Silver Lining* (New York: Revell, 1907), pp. 54-56.

6. Kenneth Wuest, "Treasures from the Greek New Testament," *Wuest's Word Studies from the Greek New Testament* (Grand Rapids: Eerdmans, 1979), pp. 21-22.

7. Octavius Winslow, *Help Heavenward* (Carlisle: Banner of Truth Trust, 2000), pp. 49-50.

8. Annie Johnson Flint, "One Day at a Time," *Best-Loved Poems* (Toronto: Evangelical Publishers, n.d.), pp. 70-71.

9. Hannah Whitall Smith, *The God of All Comfort* (Chicago: Moody Press, 1956), pp. 31, 42.

10. Leon Morris, *Revelation* (Grand Rapids: Eerdmans, 1990), p. 239.

11. George Eldon Ladd, *A Commentary on the Revelation of John* (Grand Rapids: Eerdmans, 1991), p. 29.

12. Robert H. Mounce, *The Book of Revelation* (Grand Rapids: Eerdmans, 1977), pp. 73, 374.

13. Robert G. Bratcher, *A Translator's Guide to the Revelation of John* (London: United Bible Societies, 1984), p. 12.

14. Quoted in Robert Parsons, *Quotes from the Quiet Hour* (Chicago: Moody Press, 1949), p. 42.

15. Mrs. Charles Cowman, *Streams in the Desert* (Los Angeles: Oriental Missionary Society, 1925), pp. 250-51.

16. Octavius Winslow, *Help Heavenward*, p. 29.

17. Cowman, *Streams in the Desert*, p. 251.

❦ ACKNOWLEDGMENTS ❧

I am first and foremost thankful to the Lord for entrusting to me the idea and the privilege of writing this book of quiet times.

Thank you to Bob Hawkins Jr., president of Harvest House Publishers, and to Terry Glaspey for encouraging me to write this quiet time experience. Thank you to the entire team at Harvest House Publishers, who do everything with excellence. It is an absolute privilege to serve the Lord with you. Thank you especially to Gene Skinner, my editor at Harvest House—serving the Lord with you is such a joy.

Thank you to my precious family—David, Mother, Dad, Rob, Tania, Kayla, Christopher, Eloise, Andy, Keegan, and James—for your unconditional love and encouragement as I write books and share the message that God has laid on my heart in my quiet times alone with Him. A special thanks to you, David, for your love, wisdom, and brilliance as together we run this race set before us.

I am so very thankful to our Quiet Time Ministries team for serving the Lord together with me, especially in these days when so many incredible opportunities are opening up for this ministry. Thank you Kayla Branscum, Paula Zillmer, Shirley Peters, Conni Hudson, Cindy Clark, and Kelly Abeyratne. Kayla, thank you for coming alongside me more than five years ago in Quiet Time Ministries as my assistant. You have a thousand gifts and talents that you use to the glory of God—I am so thankful to Him for you. A special thanks to Charlie Branscum, who has tirelessly served the Lord in so many ways with Quiet Time Ministries.

And then, thank you to my dear friends who have offered such words of truth, encouragement, and hope that I have needed all along the way: Beverly Trupp, Andy Graybill, Dottie McDowell, Vonette Bright, Julie Airis, Helen Peck, Stefanie Kelly, Carolyn Haynes, John and Betty Mann, Sandi Rogers, Myra Murphy, and Kathleen Otremba.

Thank you to the board of directors of Quiet Time Ministries, the *Enriching Your Quiet Time* magazine staff, and those who partner financially and prayerfully together with me in Quiet Time Ministries.

Thank you to the staff at Southwest Community Church for loving the Lord. A special thanks to Shelley Smith, the women's ministries assistant, for your tireless service and commitment to our Lord. And thank you to the women at Southwest Community Church—it is such a joy and privilege to serve the Lord together with you.

And then, thank you to those who have been such a huge help to me in the writing and publishing of books: Jim Smoke, whose advice and help have, by God's grace, completely altered the course of my life; and to Greg Johnson, my agent, who has come alongside me and Quiet Time Ministries to help us teach the goals that the Lord has laid on my heart.

Finally, thank you to all those saints who have the run the race before us and who have shown me that I could stand strong and trust God and His Word; especially Corrie ten Boom, Charles Haddon Spurgeon, John Henry Jowett, Octavius Winslow, A.W. Tozer, F.B. Meyer, G. Campbell Morgan, Amy Carmichael, and Annie Johnson Flint. May their tribe increase.

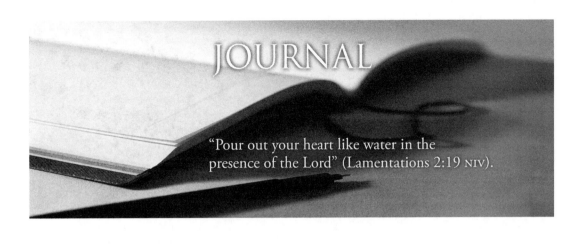

JOURNAL

"Pour out your heart like water in the presence of the Lord" (Lamentations 2:19 NIV).

JOURNAL

"Pour out your heart like water in the presence of the Lord" (Lamentations 2:19 NIV).

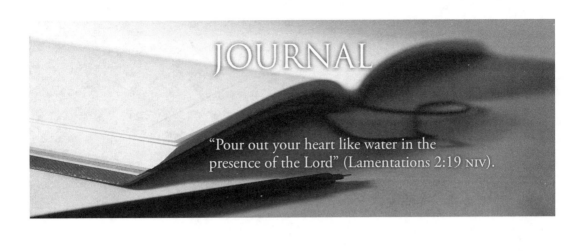

JOURNAL

"Pour out your heart like water in the presence of the Lord" (Lamentations 2:19 NIV).

....

....

....

....

....

....

....

....

....

....

....

....

....

....

....

....

....

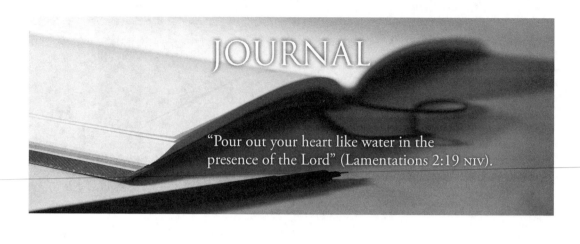

JOURNAL

"Pour out your heart like water in the presence of the Lord" (Lamentations 2:19 NIV).

....
....
....
....
....
....
....
....
....
....
....
....
....
....
....
....
....

JOURNAL

"Pour out your heart like water in the presence of the Lord" (Lamentations 2:19 NIV).

....

....

....

....

....

....

....

....

....

....

....

....

....

....

....

....

JOURNAL

"Pour out your heart like water in the presence of the Lord" (Lamentations 2:19 NIV).

ADORE GOD IN PRAYER

"Don't worry about anything;
instead, pray about everything" (Philippians 4:6 NLT).

Prayer for_____

Date: Topic:
Scripture:
Request:

Answer:

Date: Topic:
Scripture:
Request:

Answer:

Date: Topic:
Scripture:
Request:

Answer:

Date: Topic:
Scripture:
Request:

Answer:

Date: Topic:
Scripture:
Request:

Answer:

ADORE GOD IN PRAYER

"Don't worry about anything;
instead, pray about everything" (Philippians 4:6 NLT).

*Prayer for*_____

Date: Topic:
Scripture:
Request:

Answer:

Date: Topic:
Scripture:
Request:

Answer:

Date: Topic:
Scripture:
Request:

Answer:

Date: Topic:
Scripture:
Request:

Answer:

Date: Topic:
Scripture:
Request:

Answer:

ADORE GOD IN PRAYER

"Don't worry about anything;
instead, pray about everything" (Philippians 4:6 NLT).

*Prayer for*_____

Date: Topic:
Scripture:
Request:

Answer:

Date: Topic:
Scripture:
Request:

Answer:

Date: Topic:
Scripture:
Request:

Answer:

Date: Topic:
Scripture:
Request:

Answer:

Date: Topic:
Scripture:
Request:

Answer:

ADORE GOD IN PRAYER

"Don't worry about anything;
instead, pray about everything" (Philippians 4:6 NLT).

Prayer for_____

Date: Topic:
Scripture:
Request:

Answer:

_____

Date: Topic:
Scripture:
Request:

Answer:

_____

Date: Topic:
Scripture:
Request:

Answer:

_____

Date: Topic:
Scripture:
Request:

Answer:

_____

Date: Topic:
Scripture:
Request:

Answer:

_____

ADORE GOD IN PRAYER

"Don't worry about anything;
instead, pray about everything" (Philippians 4:6 NLT).

Prayer for

Date: Topic:
Scripture:
Request:

Answer:

Date: Topic:
Scripture:
Request:

Answer:

Date: Topic:
Scripture:
Request:

Answer:

Date: Topic:
Scripture:
Request:

Answer:

Date: Topic:
Scripture:
Request:

Answer:

ADORE GOD IN PRAYER

"Don't worry about anything;
instead, pray about everything" (Philippians 4:6 NLT).

*Prayer for*_____

Date: Topic:
Scripture:
Request:

Answer:

Date: Topic:
Scripture:
Request:

Answer:

Date: Topic:
Scripture:
Request:

Answer:

Date: Topic:
Scripture:
Request:

Answer:

Date: Topic:
Scripture:
Request:

Answer:
